KERRY ABÚ

THE GREAT GAELIC FOOTBALL FAN BOOK

SYLVESTER HENNESSY

MERCIER PRESS

MERCIER PRESS

Cork

www.mercierpress.ie

© Sylvester Hennessy, 2019

Foreword © Peter Keane, 2019

ISBN: 978 1 78117 665 8

A CIP record for this title is available from the British Library

Printed and bound in the EU.

CONTENTS

FOREWORD

I've always felt that, first and foremost, I am a Kerry supporter.

My earliest childhood memories go right back to the great Kerry team under Mick O'Dwyer. They were a marvellous side to watch. Our trips to Dublin to support Kerry in Croke Park as young lads were special. My father and mother instilled in me and my siblings a deep love for the GAA. But I suppose I am not the first person in Kerry to say that the GAA has defined me. After all, in a county like Kerry, football is such a rich part of so many people's lives.

Even though I was Kerry Minor manager for the past three years, I travelled to the Kerry Senior games like everyone else. Last year, I enjoyed every trip, whether it was the Clare game in Killarney, or the game down in Cork, or even up in Clones. I thought that the turnout by Kerry supporters in Clones last year was great. Equally so, there was something in excess of 20,000 people in Killarney for the Kildare game on an August weekend, despite the fact that, historically, people say this is a bad weekend for Kerry fans to attend games because of our tourist industry.

There was also huge support for every game the Kerry Minors played. Tickets were scarce for the All-Ireland Minor finals over the past three years, as Kerry were not competing in the Senior final, yet there was still massive support in Croke Park. I often wondered how those people got tickets.

I am delighted to get this opportunity to say thank you to the Kerry supporters. We have had some special days in the past, and I am hoping that there will be special days ahead.

I wish Sylvester Hennessy and Mercier Press the very best with this publication. I know Sylvester well, having worked with him for nearly a decade. He played a key role with the Kerry Minor team over the past three years. He is a man who knows his football and I can think of no better man to write a book like this.

I am sure this book will be an enjoyable read for Kerry supporters, not only here in the county, but in the four corners of Ireland and all around the world.

Peter Keane
Kerry Senior Football Manager

INTRODUCTION
KERRY GAA – IT'S IN OUR DNA

What is the secret of Kerry's football dominance over the years? No other county in Ireland can come anywhere near the footballers of the Kingdom in terms of inter-county success.

The answer is a simple one. Success breeds success, and in a land that is festooned with All-Ireland medals, Kerry footballers are expected to win All-Ireland titles. It is the natural order of things and long may this continue.

When you visit Liverpool, the city is a shrine to The Beatles and their other great passion, soccer. The same can be said of other parts of the world where a place or area is defined by sport or culture.

When you arrive in Kerry there is no mistaking the importance of Gaelic football in the county. As you approach the outskirts of the county town, Tralee, at the Clashlehane roundabout, a wonderful sculpture by Mark Rode of 4 footballers in action is your introduction to the town. Then, as you drive around the town, you come across John Joe Sheehy Road, Austin Stack Park (the headquarters of Kerry GAA), the Joe Keohane roundabout, Dan Spring Road, Bill Kinnerk Road and Bracker O'Regan Road. At one end of Bracker O'Regan Road, the Mounthawk roundabout is dedicated to Joe Barrett, while at the other the Monavalley roundabout is dedicated to John Joe 'Purty' Landers. Needless to say, all of these are named after Kerry footballing greats.

A trip around the county offers more examples of the connection between football and Kerry people, with statues of Mick O'Dwyer in Waterville, John Egan in Sneem and Páidí Ó Sé in Ventry just further illustrations of Kerry's obsession with the game.

As the Romans and the Greeks had their gods, we in the Kingdom of Kerry have our own pantheon of greats. In the Kingdom we worship our former football heroes. Football is our religion. What's more, to most Kerry people at this point, it feels like Gaelic football is part of our very DNA.

OVERVIEW

COUNTY GROUNDS

Fitzgerald Stadium

Fitzgerald Stadium is the main county ground in Kerry. The stadium is renowned for its stunning natural vistas of Killarney's mountains and is the home championship venue for the Kerry Senior football team.

The Killarney venue was named in honour of former Kerry and Dr Crokes great, Dick Fitzgerald. Fitzgerald Stadium was officially opened on 31 May 1936 by Dr Michael O'Brien, the then Bishop of Kerry, and J. M. Harty, Archbishop of Cashel.

In 1937 the new Killarney stadium played host to the All-Ireland hurling final between Tipperary and Kilkenny, due to the unavailability of Croke Park. This was at the time of the construction of the first Cusack Stand in the Dublin ground and Fitzgerald Stadium was seen as the most suitable replacement.

Further developments took place at Fitzgerald Stadium in the 1970s, with the erection of the Dr O'Sullivan Stand and a pavilion. All of this raised the capacity to 39,120.

Renovations have been ongoing ever since and the ground has had many facelifts. The laying of the current 'Prunty pitch' proved to be hugely popular and Fitzgerald Stadium now boasts one of the best playing surfaces in the GAA.

In the winter of 2008–09, the first phase in the planned redevelopment of the terraces at both ends of the pitch was finished. Among the changes was an extension of terracing at the Lewis Road end as far as the stand. The terracing is designed in such a way as to allow its continuation along the stand side if and when the stand is upgraded. The new terracing has added an additional 4,000 capacity, bringing the overall stadium capacity to 43,000. Further development is planned, which will raise this to 50,000 in the future.

There are 4 large dressing rooms underneath the new terrace with individual showering and toilet facilities. The dressing rooms are state-of-the-art and on a par with Croke Park.

There is also an area for medical and physio staff, as well as a separate area for mentors. Players exit the dressing rooms via a tunnel on the Lewis Road end of the pitch.

There are 3 levels in all underneath the new

terrace. Level 1 has the dressing rooms and shops at the rear of the terrace. Level 2 has very spacious meeting rooms for stewards, gardaí, drug testing and a press room for post-match interviews, with a stairway direct to the dressing-room area. The top level, accessed by lift or stairs, is made up of a control tower for crowd control and monitoring, and there is also a spacious room overlooking the pitch for TV match analysis.

The main entrance area from Lewis Road has been extended with facilities for selling tickets on match day. On the stand side, there are new entrance/exit stairs at the scoreboard end of the stand. New wheelchair facilities are located in the stand, with lift access. There is a new seating area for substitutes/mentors in the stand adjacent to the VIP area in the middle.

On 15 November 2016, Fitzgerald Stadium was announced as one of 12 possible venues in Ireland's bid to host the 2023 Rugby World Cup – a bid which unfortunately failed.

Fitzgerald Stadium has also been nicknamed 'Fortress Killarney', as Kerry's last loss in a Senior inter-county championship game in the stadium came back in 1995.

Austin Stack Park

Austin Stack Park is Kerry's second county ground and is in Tralee. The ground was named after Austin Stack, an Irish revolutionary and captain of the All-Ireland-winning Kerry Gaelic football team of 1904. It is situated on John Joe Sheehy Road, named after another former Kerry great.

The venue has played host to many Kerry inter-county home games at all levels, while the county championship football and hurling finals are also normally held here.

The presence of floodlights at the ground means that the venue is widely used for National League games that are played during winter and spring months, as well as for other important matches outside of the summer season.

The headquarters of Kerry GAA, the Kerry County Board has also been based in the ground since 1985. Their office is in the premises known as the 'Pavilion', which first opened back in 1967.

Both ends of the pitch have their own commonly used names. The end at the west side of the pitch used to be known as 'the Mitchels end', as it backed onto the former site of the John Mitchels GAA club. It is now often referred to as the 'Aldi end' of the field, given that an Aldi store is now situated where the Mitchels pitch used to be. It is also sometimes referred to as the 'town end'. The east side of the field is called either the 'Killarney end' or the 'Horan's end', referring to the shopping centre situated behind it.

Austin Stack Park has been used as a venue for games since the 19th century. Back then it was generally known as 'The Sportsfield' and was owned by the County Kerry Athletic and Cricket Club. At that time the pitch was oval shaped.

In 1903 the trustees of the stadium rented the ground to a committee consisting of all GAA members. The Kerry County Board then purchased the ground in 1929. In 1934 'The Sportsfield' was converted into a rectangular pitch to host the 1934 All-Ireland semi-final. It was in 1944 that the county board renamed the ground in honour of Austin Stack.

In 1994 a new development was completed, including a new stand, terracing and the redeveloped county board offices. The first Kerry GAA game played under floodlights took place there in November 2001.

In 2007 plans were approved for a replacement

stadium on a site outside the town that is currently occupied by Ballybeggan Racecourse. In December 2009, however, due to the downturn in the economy, it was announced that plans for the new stadium and development had been put on hold indefinitely.

Instead, in 2014, a committee was put in place by the county board to look into the gradual refurbishment of the existing ground. The playing surface was upgraded, a new electronic scoreboard was erected and the floodlighting system was upgraded. The terracing at the old 'Mitchels end' of the ground was also upgraded. There are plans to upgrade the press facilities and other areas of the ground in the immediate future.

Austin Stack Park remains a very popular venue with Kerry football supporters and is renowned for its match-day atmosphere, which is evident especially on county hurling final day. When Dublin visited Tralee recently for an Allianz League game, 12,000 patrons filled the stadium to capacity, its cauldron-like atmosphere very much in effect that night.

KERRY JERSEY

The Green and Gold

Kerry's traditional colours are green and gold, and the county team kits are composed of a green shirt with a single golden hoop, white shorts and green and gold socks. This hasn't always been the case, however.

In the early days of the inter-county All-Ireland Senior Football Championship, counties were represented by the club county champions. Kerry's first representatives were Laune Rangers, and so the blue of Laune Rangers was worn in Kerry's first championship outing in 1889. In fact, blue was the only colour in use between 1889 and 1895 inclusive, as the teams that went forward to represent Kerry were Laune Rangers and Ballymacelligott, who both wore the colour.

In the early 20th century, selection committees were put in place by the Kerry County Board. Tralee Mitchels were the dominant force in the county championship at the time; accordingly, they had an influential voice in the selection of the team. Given the Mitchels' success and influence, the county footballers ended up wearing the Mitchels' colours of green and gold.

Things did not always go to plan, however. There are conflicting accounts of the jersey that Kerry wore in the first of the three games of the infamous 1903 All-Ireland Senior Football Championship Final series with Kildare, but the predominant colour of the jersey was undoubtedly red according to most accounts that exist of the game. One source says that it was a red jersey with green neck and cuffs, which were the colours of the Tralee Mitchels junior football team. Another says that it was an entirely red jersey with no green in it. The reason that Kerry wore this red or mainly red jersey was that a new set of green and gold jerseys that they had ordered was not delivered in time for the game.

For the later games in the 1903 series of finals, however, Kerry wore green jerseys with gold on the cuffs and over the shoulders. And green and gold have been Kerry's traditional colours from this 1903 triumph onward.

The 'classic' style is green with a gold hoop. The colours have rarely changed. In the 1939 All-Ireland Senior Football Championship Final, however, Kerry played Meath, who also wear green and gold. To avoid a colour clash, Kerry wore the red and white of Dingle, the county champions at the time. This was also done in the 1980s finals against Offaly to avoid colour clashes.

Nowadays, the Kerry Seniors change kit is usually blue, reflecting the Munster GAA colours. However, we have seen other changed strips throughout the years. Former Kerry player and fashion designer Paul Galvin, for example, designed a new 'back to gold' away strip in 2018.

Kerry's inter-county teams are sponsored by the Kerry Group, and this is one of the longest-standing sponsorship arrangements in the GAA, the teams having been connected with Kerry Group since sponsorship became more open in the GAA in the early 1990s.

Kerry GAA Crest

Kerry inter-county teams first wore a crest on their jerseys in the Centenary All-Ireland final win over Dublin back in 1984.

The crest was originally shaped like a shield with a green background and gold trimming. *Ciarraí* was positioned on top of the crest and then the main body had 3 designs: crossed hurleys and 2 sliotars to represent hurling; a football illustrated in dot style to represent football, and a hand and ball to represent handball. This was used until 1988 when a new Kerry crest was designed.

The new crest was used from 1988 to 2011 and was based more on Irish and Celtic symbolism, featuring a round tower, an Irish wolfhound and a harp, with the sea, mountains and a map of Kerry in the background.

The current Kerry crest came into use in 2012. Initially there was a mixed reaction to it, but as time has gone by the new-look crest has proven to be very popular. It features design elements that represent Kerry's people, landscape, flora, fauna and artistry. These include:

- A bold Celtic-style *Ciarraí* brand, featuring a crowned C, which pays homage to the county's moniker: 'The Kingdom'.
- The *naomhóg* (a craft associated with the coastal communities around Kerry), propelled by a sail featuring a Celtic cross, which is the symbol of the GAA. This image also calls to mind one of Kerry's

most famous sons, St Brendan, and his epic voyage.

- A red deer (*Fia Rua*). This is Ireland's largest wild animal, whose only remaining native herd is found on the slopes of Torc and Mangerton in Killarney National Park. These animals are believed to have had a continuous presence in Ireland since the end of the last Ice Age (*c.* 10,000 BC) and are steeped in folklore. It is said that 'Tuan', the King of the Deer, was given rights of free passage by Fionn MacCumhail to the mountains of Kerry and that his bloodline lives on in the present herd.

- Skellig Michael's iconic silhouette rising out of the Atlantic Ocean. This is a designated UNESCO World Heritage site and is famous around the globe.

- A Killarney woodland fern, which thrives in wild places. It is an evocation of the county's majestic mountains, valleys and hills.

- A storm petrel (*An Guairdeall*). Kerry plays host to the largest numbers of this species anywhere in the world.

– A background pattern of concentric circles, inspired by the gilding on the Ballinclemisig 'gold box' (part of the 'Kerry gold hoard' in the National Museum) and by the Bronze Age stone carvings found all over Kerry.

The new Kerry crest now takes pride of place on all Kerry GAA merchandise. And while the round tower and wolfhound motif found in the previous crest were hugely popular, the new design has become part and parcel of Kerry GAA life and is universally accepted.

82 ALL-IRELAND INTER-COUNTY TITLES

Before delving into the history of the Kerry GAA, let's look at the hard facts behind the Kingdom's footballing success. If we look at the 4 grades in inter-county football – Senior, Junior, U–21/U–20, and Minor, Kerry have won a phenomenal 82 All-Ireland football titles. That's 37 Senior, 19 Junior, 10 U–21 and 16 Minor.

That is 32 football titles more than Dublin, who play second fiddle to Kerry in the overall table. Dublin have won 28 Senior, 6 Junior, 5 U–21 and 11 Minor, which totals 50 All-Ireland football titles.

Cork are third in the overall table with 7 Senior, 17 Junior, 11 U–21 and 10 Minor, which totals 45 All-Ireland football titles.

Facts are facts. Kerry are the most successful county in the history of Gaelic football. Footballers from the 'Kingdom' top nearly all the all-time-winners lists across the various age groups and grades.

Specifically in the All-Ireland Senior Football

Championship, Kerry's record of 37 titles puts them 9 ahead of Dublin, who have won 28. So it's clear that, despite Dublin's recent success, they are still some distance behind Kerry's record at Senior level.

Kerry have also contested 59 All-Ireland Senior Football Championship finals, with Dublin once again being the next highest participator with 41 appearances.

Kerry are also top of the Junior and Minor all-time winners list. It is only at U–21/U–20 level that Kerry lie one behind another county, with Cork on 11 titles to the Kingdom's 10.

In Ladies football, Kerry also hold the all-time All-Ireland Senior winners record, with 11 titles alongside neighbours Cork.

It is clear that, across all codes, Kerry football is undoubtedly to the fore in terms of success and pedigree. It is surprising, therefore, to learn that Kerry's proud Gaelic football tradition actually grew out of quite humble beginnings.

THE FOUNDING AND EARLY HISTORY OF KERRY GAA

HUMBLE BEGINNINGS:
THE BIRTH OF KERRY GAA

Most people will be aware that the GAA was formed in 1884. Research suggests that the GAA was introduced to Kerry in 1885. The first big event was the Tralee GAA sports meeting on 17 June 1885, organised by Michael Cusack. A major success, this helped establish the GAA's control over athletics across Ireland.

In November 1887, the Tralee branch of the GAA was formed by Maurice Moynihan, a member of the IRB and a well-known Irish nationalist.

The following year, in November 1888, Kerry's first annual GAA convention was held and the Kerry County Board was inaugurated. Moynihan was elected secretary, with Thomas Slattery, an IRB leader in Tralee and a republican from Rock Street, elected as president. By the end of 1888, 19 hurling and football clubs were affiliated with the Kerry Board; this would grow to 33 by the end of 1889.

The inaugural Kerry county championships began in 1889, with clubs like Killorglin's Laune Rangers, Ballymacelligott, Killarney Crokes and

Tralee Mitchels participating. In total, 15 football and 5 hurling teams competed in this inaugural championship.

The first ever club championship matches were held on 3 March 1889. They were a triple header in a field used by the Killarney GAA club a mile from the town. Laune Rangers played Barraduff O'Connells in the first ever match.

On 19 May, Kenmare became hurling champions, beating a fancied Kilmoyley team in the final.

On 26 May, Laune Rangers won the inaugural football championship, beating Killarney Crokes in the final in Tralee.

***

As the GAA grew within Kerry, it faced several problems.

Remember, the establishment of the GAA back in 1884 coincided with a time when anything that was seen to celebrate Irish culture and tradition was treated with suspicion by the ruling British government and their officials. Membership of the GAA was therefore viewed as a blatant and provocative expression of Irish nationalism, and consequently of independent thinking.

And there is no doubt that politics and football in Kerry did go hand in hand around that time. After all, leading figures in Kerry GAA like Maurice Moynihan and Thomas Slattery were also prominent figures in the Irish nationalist movement.

However, suspicion did not come exclusively from the British government and its officials. The clergy, who were also a dominant force in the county at the time, disapproved in the main of the GAA. In fact, it would be fair to say that they were very much pro-establishment. The presence of known IRB leaders at the head of the Kerry GAA meant that the Church was apprehensive of this fledgling organisation and its potential influence on their parishioners.

However, it was not just those in a position of authority who threatened the flourishing of the GAA within Kerry. Economic problems in the late 1880s and early 1890s also had a massive impact on the GAA, as the need to work and feed families became a much more pressing matter to the Kerry people than playing sports and asserting their national identity.

There were also huge problems with violence

in the games themselves in the embryonic stages of the Kerry GAA, and the local championships seemed to be rife with match-day brawls.

Added to this was the problem of competition from other sports, such as rugby and athletics, which continued to be very popular in Kerry during the period. At the time, the GAA had a ban on its members playing 'foreign' sports. The likes of rugby, soccer and cricket were all viewed by the Irish nationalists within the GAA as games that had been invented and played by their British rulers and oppressors. Young athletic Irish men were therefore encouraged to play their national sports as an expression of their 'Irishness'.

This ban on foreign games made it almost impossible for young Irish men to play any sport other than Gaelic games. If they were caught playing a 'foreign' sport, they were subsequently banned from playing Gaelic games for a period of time.

In Dr Richard McElligott's brilliant analysis of the foundations of Kerry GAA, *Forging A Kingdom: The GAA in Kerry 1884–1934*, he highlights a number of issues that arose in the early days of the GAA which are still topical today.

There was, for example, the need for an open draw in the championship to counter Kerry's – and to a lesser extent, Cork's – dominance in Munster. Prior to this change, Kerry and Cork had been seeded in the draw, which gave them an advantage, as by avoiding each other they were almost guaranteed to reach the Munster final year in, year out.

Professionalism was also a concern, as was the loss of players to emigration – an issue that has continued to be a grave worry for Kerry throughout the history of the GAA, with some rural clubs struggling to field full teams, while other clubs have even been forced into merging with neighbouring clubs in order to survive.

Despite all these problems, the nascent organisation continued to grow in Kerry, and it wasn't long before Kerry had its first national success. Surprisingly – at least for the modern reader – this did not occur in football. Instead, it was hurling that brought Kerry its first All-Ireland title.

ALL-IRELAND HURLING TITLE

In May 1891 Ballyduff became the county hurling champions, beating Kilmoyley in the final. The tradition at the time in the GAA was that the county champions would represent their county in the Munster and All-Ireland series. This process continued into the early part of the 20th century, until it was decided that Kerry would field inter-county teams that drew from the best players throughout the county and not just from the county championship-winning team.

After a shock win in the Munster semi-final over Cork champions Blackrock, the Kerry hurlers faced the Limerick champions, Treaty Stones, in Newcastle West in December 1891 in the Munster final.

Kerry actually lost the final by a point, but they appealed the decision to the GAA's Central Council, arguing that the referee had unfairly disallowed an equalising point scored just before full time. The appeal was successful and Ballyduff won the replayed final, becoming the only Kerry side to win a Munster title. The replay score was

2–4 to 0–1, with the game played in Abbeyfeale in January 1892.

Ballyduff encountered Wexford's Crossabeg club in the All-Ireland final, which was played on 28 February 1892 in Clonturk Park (near Drumcondra) in Dublin. With the sides level, Crossabeg won a free and seemed to score a winning point, but the referee declared that he'd called full time before the ball sailed over the bar. Once again, luck was on the Kerry team's side.

Ballyduff went on to win the game in extra time on a scoreline of 2–3 to 1–5.

Kerry were All-Ireland champions for the very first time. And it was in hurling.

It has remained the county's only All-Ireland Senior Hurling title. In Kerry right now there are only 8 Senior hurling clubs that come from a hinterland just north of Tralee, running from the Stacks Mountains to the Cashen Bridge that borders Ballyduff and Ballybunion. These 8 clubs of Abbeydorney, Crotta O'Neill's, Lixnaw, Ballyduff, Causeway, Ballyheigue, Kilmoyley and St Brendan's have backboned Kerry hurling for the past 130 years.

There are other pockets of hurling in the

county, however. Kenmare and Kilgarvan in particular have a real tradition, while Tralee town and Killarney have also sustained hurling teams, and Duagh has also developed a hurling team.

Despite this, the number one game in the county of Kerry remains Gaelic football, and that is reflected in the fact that the game is played in all 4 corners of the county.

THE FALL AND RISE OF
KERRY GAA AT THE TURN
OF THE 20TH CENTURY

Kerry's first All-Ireland football final appearance came in 1893 with the Laune Rangers club from Killorglin town. They met Dublin's Young Irelanders in Clonturk on 26 March 1893, and lost that final 1–4 to 0–3. This was to be the last appearance by a Kerry team in an All-Ireland final for 12 years, as football and hurling declined in popularity in the county.

In the 1890s, because of a widespread economic recession in the country and the re-emergence of mass emigration, the GAA took a back seat in people's everyday lives in Kerry. The county's geographical isolation on the south-western seaboard was a major factor.

In 1896, due to the diminishing number of its members, the GAA revoked its previous ban on members playing foreign sports in order to stem its decline in the county. However, this did little to halt the damage. In 1897, Thomas Slattery retired as president of Kerry GAA, further damaging its popularity. In fact, the GAA in Kerry practically ceased to exist in the absence of their energetic leader.

At the turn of the century, things slowly began to improve. In 1900, a Listowel journalist by the name of Thomas F. O'Sullivan proved to be the catalyst for the revival in Kerry GAA's fortunes. O'Sullivan used his platform as a journalist to make an appeal through the local press to re-form the Kerry County Board. The GAA's central council helped him to organise a Kerry GAA convention in May 1900, and at this event O'Sullivan was elected secretary of the new Kerry County Board. By the end of the year, 30 clubs had re-formed and reaffiliated to the new board.

Austin Stack was another pivotal figure in Kerry GAA at the time, and was instrumental in the surge for success on the national stage by the Kerry football team just after the turn of the century. While still a player, Stack became secretary of the re-formed Tralee Mitchels GAA club in 1902 and was also elected onto the county board. Mitchels dominated the local county championship during this period, winning 9 titles in a row.

In October 1904 Kerry won only their second Munster title, when Mitchels beat the Cork champions Lees 1–7 to 0–3 in what was the 1903 Munster final. They beat Mayo in the semi-final to reach the 1903 All-Ireland 'Home' Final against Kildare (though played on 23 July 1905).

This final ended up capturing the Irish sporting public's imagination. The reason that there was such a huge interest in this was that it took 3 games to provide a winner.

The first game was played in Thurles on 23 July 1905. Kildare were leading by 1–3 to 0–4 with 5 minutes remaining, when an apparent Kerry goal – scored after the Kildare goalkeeper, Jack Fitzgerald, was believed to be behind the line as he fielded a free – was disputed. The crowd invaded the pitch when the 'own goal' was disallowed, meaning that the game eventually had to be abandoned.

The re-scheduled game took place in Cork on 28 August. The teams finished level (Kerry 0–7, Kildare 1–4), with Joyce Condon getting the crucial goal for Kildare to secure the draw.

The third and deciding match was played in Cork on 15 October on an extremely wet day, with Kerry winning their first All-Ireland 'Home' final by 0–8 to 0–2 in front of 20,000 people, a massive crowd for the time.

Kerry subsequently beat London, who were captained by Sam Maguire, in the actual, or what was sometimes referred to as the 'Away', All-Ireland final on a scoreline of 0–11 to 0–03. This two-final format occurred during this period because London were given a bye to the All-Ireland final in the hope that this would assist in the development of the GAA in London. However, given that this was London's fourth heavy defeat in a row in a final, the 1903 final ended up being the last time that this 'bye' format was used.

The following year, Kerry retained their title. In what was the 1904 final (though played on 1 July 1906), Kerry recorded their first win over Dublin in the All-Ireland final on a scoreline of 0–5 to 0–2. Dick Fitzgerald proved to be the hero of the game, scoring the only point of the second half in a final that was played in front of 10,000 people in Cork.

After a difficult period, the Kingdom's fortunes had risen. However, other challenging times lay ahead.

A WAR-TORN
AND DIVIDED KINGDOM

The War of Independence commenced in 1919. From *Forging a Kingdom*, Dr Richard McElligott's book, we learn that many local GAA members in Kerry became heavily involved in the fighting.

When local Irish Volunteer companies re-organised into an IRA brigade structure in 1919, Patrick Cahill of Mitchels took charge of the Kerry No. 1 Brigade, which oversaw the north and west of the county. Tadhg Kennedy of the Kerry County Board became the chief IRA intelligence officer for the Kerry region during the conflict, often working closely with Michael Collins. Paddy Landers, who played with Kerry, became the commanding officer of the Listowel Company, a battalion of Kerry No. 1 Brigade. Humphrey Murphy of Kerry and Dr Crokes was the O/C of the Kerry No. 2 Brigade, which consisted of the southern and eastern battalions. Fellow club man John Joe Rice commanded one of these battalions, overseeing the 3rd Battalion in the Kenmare district.

Future Kerry captain Con Brosnan of Newtownsandes GAA was said to be involved in the assassination of Royal Irish Constabulary District Inspector Tobias O'Sullivan in January 1921 in Listowel. Another future Kerry captain, John Joe Sheehy, was the Tralee IRA commander during the war.

Due to this turbulent period, the Munster Championship of 1920 was delayed and not played for a couple of years. The 1921 Munster Championship was not played at all.

As we can only imagine, the Civil War that followed on from the War of Independence had a very divisive effect in the county, and the GAA was of course hit badly by the conflict. On either side stood divided families, friends and team mates. Kerry lost the delayed 1920 Munster final, which was played in 1922, as they were missing a number of players who were either interned for their involvement with the republican movement, or part of the Free State Army. The county also lost the delayed 1922 Munster final for similar reasons.

When it came to competing on the provincial and national stage, Kerry needed to get their act together.

HEALING THE WOUNDS
OF THE CIVIL WAR

At the end of the Civil War, Kerry GAA quickly needed to reorganise itself. Some progress seemed to be made in 1923 when Kerry played in the Munster Championship and beat Limerick and then Tipperary in the 1923 final. Yet all was still not right, both within the county and in the county team itself. After all, hundreds of IRA men from Kerry were still interned over their role in the conflict. They included many of Kerry's best players, such as Joe Barrett.

In December 1923, many of the internees were released. In January 1924, a team made up of Kerry ex-internee footballers challenged the Kerry Senior team to a match.

Both teams trained hard and there was huge local media interest in the event, as it was announced the match would serve as a trial for places on the Kerry side that was due to play Cavan in the All-Ireland semi-final that year.

The game was held in February and the official Kerry side won what was reported at the time to be a tight, rough match by 0–5 to 1–0.

Afterwards, there was an agreement between both parties that a re-match would take place and this time around, on 23 March, the internees recorded a comprehensive win on a scoreline of 4–4 to 0–4.

After those infamous encounters, a Kerry team made its first appearance in Croke Park in 5 years, composed of players from both sides. It was a hugely symbolic moment; despite their political divides, Kerry players were now united under one jersey.

The team lost to Dublin in what was the 1923 All-Ireland final that September by 1–5 to 1–3. However, within 6 months, they denied Dublin a 4-in-a-row, winning the final of 1924 on 26 April 1925 by 0–4 to 0–3.

This great Kerry side played a huge part in healing the wounds and divisions in Kerry society after what had been a bitter Civil War. Across Ireland they became a great symbol for what could be achieved by reconciliation rather than continued division, as diehard republicans like John Joe Sheehy and Joe Barrett lined out shoulder to shoulder with Free State soldiers like Con Brosnan.

This reconciliation was sealed forever in 1931. Joe Barrett was chosen to captain Kerry for a second time that year. Instead, he offered the captaincy to Brosnan, his old war-time adversary, who was coming to the end of his distinguished career. Brosnan went on to lift the Sam Maguire Cup in September 1931. This is still seen by many as one of the most significant moments in the history of Kerry GAA.

Kerry went on to complete their first 4-in-a-row of All-Ireland Senior titles in 1932, with Joe Barrett back in the role of captain that year.

The full-back could have been captain for 3 of the 4 years of that 4-in-a-row triumph, which would also have made him the only Kerry player to captain Kerry to All-Ireland Senior glory on 3 separate occasions. His now-legendary gesture is seen by many as one of the most selfless acts in the history of the GAA.

In the process, this team became one of the greatest teams in the history of the GAA. Between 1923 and 1933, the county team won 6 Senior All-Ireland titles, 10 Munster titles and 4 National Leagues.

After a turbulent first 50 years of life in the

county, the GAA was now firmly established in Kerry.

ALL-IRELAND
INTER-COUNTY
CHAMPIONSHIP

KERRY'S ALL-IRELAND SENIOR SUCCESS

Kerry have won 37 All-Ireland Senior Football titles and that is, of course, a record. As it stands, Dublin are the county closest to Kerry in terms of All-Ireland titles won, with 28.

The county-by-county guide to All-Ireland Senior Football title winners is as follows:

Kerry (37), Dublin (28), Galway (9), Cork, Meath (7), Cavan, Wexford, Down (5), Kildare, Tipperary (4), Mayo, Offaly, Louth, Tyrone (3), Donegal, Limerick, Roscommon (2), Armagh, Derry (1)

As you can see, there is a huge disparity between Kerry and Dublin and the rest of the counties combined. There have been 131 All-Ireland Senior Football finals played in total and Kerry's 37 wins make up 28.24% of all the titles on offer. That is just over 1 in every 4 titles.

Even more revealing is the fact that Kerry have played in 59 finals in total, which is 45.7% of the finals. Basically, Kerry have been involved in nearly half of the finals on offer since they began back in 1887.

Kerry's 37 All-Ireland Senior Football Titles

1903–04, 1909, 1913–14, 1924, 1926, 1929–32, 1937, 1939–41, 1946, 1953, 1955, 1959, 1962, 1969–70, 1975, 1978–81, 1984–86, 1997, 2000, 2004, 2006–07, 2009, 2014

80 MUNSTER SENIOR FOOTBALL TITLES

The first Munster Senior Football final to be played was in 1889, with Tipperary beating Cork by 0–3 to 0–2; however, Tipperary had in fact been awarded the 1888 title prior to this, after receiving a walkover from Limerick in the final.

Kerry's first Munster Senior Football final appearance came in 1890 when they lost to Cork by 1–4 to 0–1. They met again in the 1892 final and this time around Kerry triumphed on a scoreline of 3–6 to 0–5 to capture their first Munster Senior Football title.

Since then Kerry have gone on to dominate the competition, winning their 80th Munster Senior title in 2018.

Kerry have won an 8-in-a-row of Munster Senior titles on 2 occasions: 1958–65 and 1975–82.

Kerry won 9 Munster Senior titles in the 1930s and if they capture the 2019 title they will repeat that feat this decade. Kerry will also be attempting to win a seventh Munster Senior title in a row in 2019.

Munster Title Winners

Kerry (80)

Cork (37)

Tipperary (9)

Clare (2)

Limerick (1)

Waterford (1)

Kerry's 80 Titles

1892, 1903–05, 1908–10, 1912–15, 1919, 1923–27, 1929–34, 1936–42, 1944, 1946–48, 1950–51, 1953–55, 1958–65, 1968–70, 1972, 1975–82, 1984–86, 1991, 1996–98, 2000–01, 2003–05, 2007, 2010–11, 2013–18

KERRY CAPTAINS

Thirty-three men have had the honour of captaining Kerry to All-Ireland Senior glory. Dick Fitzgerald, John Joe Sheehy, Joe Barrett and Declan O'Sullivan are the 4 men who have managed to do so twice. Fitzgerald and O'Sullivan are the only 2 Kerry men who have captained Kerry to back-to-back All-Ireland Senior inter-county triumphs.

The Kerry Senior Football captain is nominated by the Senior county championship winners in Kerry. If, for example, a club team like Dr Crokes wins the county title, then they will nominate a player from their club who is involved with the Senior inter-county team.

If a District side like East or South Kerry win, however, then things become a little more complicated. A District side is made up of several clubs and so, normally, the club from that district that wins their District Championship that year will then get to nominate the Kerry captain.

As an example of how this works, the last District side to win a county championship in

Kerry was South Kerry in 2015. St Mary's from Cahersiveen won the South Kerry Championship in 2015 and so they had the honour of nominating the Kerry captain. They chose their own club man, Bryan Sheehan, who then proceeded to captain Kerry in 2016.

While this method of selecting the Kerry captain has come under scrutiny in recent years, it has proven to be pretty equitable. There have been 18 different clubs and District teams who have had All-Ireland-winning captains come from their ranks over the years. The following is a breakdown of the spread of Kerry's 37 All-Ireland-winning captains, which, as you can see, have been pretty evenly spread across all corners of Kerry.

4 – Austin Stacks

3 – Dr Crokes, Tralee Mitchels, John Mitchels, South Kerry, Kerins O'Rahillys, East Kerry

2 – Kenmare, Dingle, West Kerry, Feale Rangers

1 – Shannon Rangers, Geraldines, Mid Kerry, An Ghaeltacht, Laune Rangers, Moyvane, Gneeveguilla

List of All-Ireland Senior Winning Kerry Captains

2014   Fionn Fitzgerald (Dr Crokes)

2009   Darran O'Sullivan (Mid Kerry)

2007   Declan O'Sullivan (South Kerry)

2006   Declan O'Sullivan (South Kerry)

2004   Dara Ó Cinnéide (An Ghaeltacht)

2000   Seamus Moynihan (East Kerry)

1997   Liam Hassett (Laune Rangers)

1986   Tommy Doyle (West Kerry)

1985   Páidí Ó Sé (West Kerry)

1984   Ambrose O'Donovan (Gneeveguilla)

1981   Jimmy Deenihan (Feale Rangers)

1980   Ger Power (Austin Stacks)

1979   Tim Kennelly (Feale Rangers)

1978   Denis 'Ogie' Moran (Shannon Rangers)

1975   Mickey Ned O'Sullivan (Kenmare)

1970   Donie O'Sullivan (East Kerry)

1969   Johnny Culloty (East Kerry)

1962   Sean Óg Sheehy (John Mitchels)

1959	Mick O'Connell (South Kerry)
1955	John Dowling (Kerins O'Rahillys)
1953	James Murphy (Kerins O'Rahillys)
1946	Paddy Kennedy (Geraldines)
1941	Bill Dillon (Dingle)
1940	Dan Spring (Kerins O'Rahillys)
1939	Tom 'Gega' O'Connor (Dingle)
1937	Miko Doyle (Austin Stacks)
1932	Joe Barrett (Austin Stacks)
1931	Con Brosnan (Moyvane)
1930	John Joe Sheehy (John Mitchels)
1929	Joe Barrett (Austin Stacks)
1926	John Joe Sheehy (John Mitchels)
1924	Phil O'Sullivan (Kenmare)
1914	Dick Fitzgerald (Dr Crokes)
1913	Dick Fitzgerald (Dr Crokes)
1909	Tom Costelloe (Tralee Mitchels)
1904	Austin Stack (Tralee Mitchels)
1903	Thady O'Gorman (Tralee Mitchels)

The Captains 15

Johnny Culloty
(1969)

Jimmy Deenihan   Joe Barrett   Donie O'Sullivan
(1981)   (1929, 1932)   (1970)

Páidí Ó Sé   Tim Kennelly   Seamus Moynihan
(1985)   (1979)   (2000)

Mick O'Connell   Paddy Kennedy
(1959)   (1946)

Ger Power   Declan O'Sullivan   Tom 'Gega'
(1980)   (2006–07)   O'Connor
     (1939)

Dara Ó Cinnéide   John Joe Sheehy   Dick Fitzgerald
(2004)   (1926, 1930)   (1913–14)

CAPTAINS' CONNECTIONS

The following is a list of Kerry inter-county football captains who had family links.

Brothers

2018
Shane Murphy   Senior Munster Champions

2018
Kieran Murphy   Junior Munster Champions

1996 /1997
Liam Hassett   U–21 Munster/All-Ireland Champions

1997
Mike Hassett   Senior Munster Champions

1983
Johnny Doyle   Junior Munster and All-Ireland Champions

1986
Tommy Doyle   Senior Munster and All-Ireland Champions

1958
Dave Geaney   Minor Munster Champions

1965
Dick Geaney   Minor Munster Champions

1947
Denny Lyne   Senior Munster Champions
1950
Jackie Lyne   Senior Munster Champions

1944
Paddy 'Bawn' Brosnan   Senior Munster Champions
1941
Tim Brosnan Junior   Munster and All-Ireland
                          Champions

Father and Sons

1979
Tim Kennelly   Munster and All-Ireland
                          Champions

1999
Noel Kennelly   U–21 Munster Champions

1931
Con Brosnan   Senior Munster and
                          All-Ireland Champions

1950
Mick Brosnan   Minor Munster and
                          All-Ireland Champions

1929/1932
Joe Barrett

Senior All-Ireland Champions/
Senior Munster and All-Ireland
Champions

1954
Tim Barrett

Minor Munster Champions

1930
John Joe Sheehy

Senior Munster and
All-Ireland Champions

1953 & 1960
Paudie Sheehy

Senior Munster Champions

1961 & 1964
Niall Sheehy

Senior Munster Champions

1962
Sean Óg Sheehy

Senior Munster and
All-Ireland Champions

1903
Thady Gorman

Senior Munster and
All-Ireland Champions

1931
Jimmy 'Gawksie'
Gorman

Minor Munster and
All-Ireland Champions

TOP KERRY GOALSCORERS IN SENIOR CHAMPIONSHIP FOOTBALL

A goalscorer is worth his weight in gold in the world of Gaelic football. Kerry have had many fine exponents of the art of goalscoring but none came anywhere near the Tralee maestro Mikey Sheehy.

Sheehy sits atop the all-time Kerry goalscorer list with 29 goals in 49 games. That's some record! He also holds the all-time record for goals scored in the history of the All-Ireland Senior Football Championship.

The Stacks legend scored more goals than any other player in the 130-year history of the championship. He also managed to do so in just 49 championship appearances, which was an average of more than 1 goal every 2 games.

Pat Spillane's record of 19 goals is also impressive, especially as he played as a wing forward. With Kieran Donaghy's retirement from inter-county football in 2018, no current player now features in the top 10.

1	Mikey Sheehy	29 (49)
2	Colm Cooper	23 (85)
3	Eoin Liston	20 (39)
4	Pat Spillane	19 (56)
5	Eoin Brosnan	15 (69)
6	John Egan	14 (41)
7	Ger Power	14 (52)
8	Kieran Donaghy	14 (69)
9	Maurice Fitzgerald	12 (45)
10	John Crowley	12 (46)

TOP SENIOR CHAMPIONSHIP APPEARANCES FOR KERRY

It probably comes as no surprise that nearly all of the players who have made 60 championship appearances or more are from the modern, Qualifier era.

The legendary Dan O'Keeffe and Dick Fitzgerald are the only non-modern-day players to make the list, and even Dan O'Keeffe was recently ousted from the top 10 when Kieran Donaghy leapfrogged him in the pantheon of greats. The Tralee man finished the season in 2018 with 69 championship appearances.

Siblings Marc and Tomás Ó Sé top the overall Kerry list with 88 Senior championship appearances each and they have only been surpassed in the all-time national list by the recently retired Sean Cavanagh from Tyrone and Stephen Cluxton from Dublin, who sits atop the all-time list.

It is not unusual to see a keeper topping appearances lists as their careers generally go on for longer than outfield players. Cluxton has made 97 championship appearances to date and could break the 100 appearance barrier if, as expected, he continues to play in goal for Dublin in 2019.

To settle the debate as to who has made the most Senior appearances for Kerry we can also introduce the League tallies. In that regard Tomás Ó Sé stands out, having made a combined 199 Senior League and championship appearances for Kerry. Second is Darragh Ó Sé with 192 appearances and third overall is of course the third member of the famed Ó Sé brothers, Marc, with 177 League and championship appearances.

Without doubt, the Ó Sé siblings from Ventry were the 'men for all seasons'.

Top Senior Championship Appearances for Kerry

1	Tomás and Marc Ó Sé	88
3	Colm Cooper	85
4	Darragh Ó Sé	81
5	Tom O'Sullivan	77
6	Declan O'Sullivan	70
6	Aidan O'Mahony	70
6	Darran O'Sullivan	70

9	Eoin Brosnan	69
9	Kieran Donaghy	69
11	Dan O'Keeffe	66
12	Bryan Sheehan	65
13	Killian Young	62
14	Seamus Moynihan	61
15	Dick Fitzgerald	58
15	Paul Galvin	58

All-Time Senior Championship Appearances

1	Stephen Cluxton	Dublin	97	2001–
2	Sean Cavanagh	Tyrone	89	2002–2017
3	Marc Ó Sé	Kerry	88	2002–2015
3	Tomás Ó Sé	Kerry	88	1998–2013
5	Colm Cooper	Kerry	85	2002–2016
6	Darragh Ó Sé	Kerry	81	1997–2009
7	Tom O'Sullivan	Kerry	76	2000–2011
8	Conor Gormley	Tyrone	75	2001–2014
8	Andy Moran	Mayo	75	2004–

10	Brian Dooher	Tyrone	73	1995–2011
11	Ross Munnelly	Laois	70	2003–
11	John O'Leary	Dublin	70	1980–1997
11	Declan O'Sullivan	Kerry	70	2003–2014
11	Aidan O'Mahony	Kerry	70	2004–2017
11	Darran O'Sullivan	Kerry	70	2005–2018

Team of Kerry Players with over 50 Championship Appearances

Dan O'Keeffe
(66)

| Marc Ó Sé | Seamus Moynihan | Tom O'Sullivan |
| (88) | (61) | (76) |

| Páidí Ó Sé | Aidan O'Mahony | Tomás Ó Sé |
| (53) | (70) | (88) |

Darragh Ó Sé   Mick O'Connell
(81)   (56)

| Jack O'Shea | Declan O'Sullivan | Pat Spillane |
| (53) | (70) | (56) |

| Colm Cooper | Kieran Donaghy | Mike Frank Russell |
| (85) | (69) | (56) |

ALL-TIME TOP SENIOR FOOTBALL CHAMPIONSHIP SCORERS

Kerry's Colm Cooper sits at the top of the pile at present. However, with teams playing more and more championship games in a season, these records are set to be smashed in the coming years. The advent of the Super 8s in particular means that teams will be playing more championship games than ever before.

Take Tyrone in 2018 as an example. In the old system, prior to the introduction of the Qualifiers, Tyrone would have exited the championship having lost their first game in Ulster to Monaghan. Instead they went on to play 10 championship games in total, coming through the Qualifiers and Super 8s to make it all the way to the All-Ireland final.

Top All-Ireland Championship Scorers

1	Colm Cooper (Kerry)	23–283 (352)	85 games 2002–2017
2	Cillian O'Connor (Mayo)	23–272 (341)	48 games 2011–

3	Mikey Sheehy (Mayo)	29–205 (292)	49 games 1973–1988
4	John Doyle (Kildare)	8–260 (284)	67 games 1999–2014
5	Padraig Joyce (Galway)	12–229 (265)	66 games 1997–2012
6	Bernard Brogan (Dublin)	21–196 (259)	58 games 2006–
7	Paddy Bradley (Derry)	17–202 (253)	44 games 1999–2012
8	Steven McDonnell (Armagh)	18–197 (251)	67 games 1999–2011
9	Maurice Fitzgerald (Kerry)	12–205 (241)	45 games 1988–2001
10	Brian Stafford (Meath)	9–206 (233)	41 games 1986–1995

KERRY'S FORTRESS:
A 24-YEAR UNBEATEN HOME RUN

Kerry's 34-game unbeaten home run in the Senior Football Championship stretches back to 23 July 1995 when Cork defeated them in the Munster final by 0–15 to 1–9.

Since then Kerry have played 9 different counties in 24 years and have managed to maintain their impeccable and unprecedented unbeaten home record.

They have played Cork (13 times), Tipperary (7), Clare and Limerick (4), Waterford (2), and Kildare, Tyrone, Sligo and Longford (1) in that period.

In those 24 years Kerry have competed in 12 All-Ireland Senior finals, winning 7 titles along the way.

Incredibly, Cork have failed to beat Kerry in the championship in their 13 visits across the county bounds in that 24-year period. Fitzgerald Stadium has become a 'house of horrors' for the Rebel hordes.

You would have to have been born before 1990 to realistically have any memory of the last time

Kerry lost a championship game on Kerry soil. Accordingly not many of the Kerry Senior Football panel will even remember what it is like to see Kerry lose a championship game on their own turf.

With the advent of the Super 8s it will be interesting to see how much longer Kerry can keep this winning home run going. In 2019 Kerry's only likely home game will come in the Super 8s – if they manage to qualify for that stage of the championship.

While the GAA does not have a definitive set of all-time records for some reason, we can confirm without any fear of contradiction that the 34-game, 24-year run is the longest unbeaten championship run at home in the history of the Senior Football Championship. In fact, it is likely that no team has come anywhere near this record.

In any other sport this record would be recognised in some official capacity, but that, unfortunately, is not the GAA's style.

Kerry scored a pretty impressive 44–544 and conceded 20–341 in those 34 games, which is an average score per game of 1–17 with an average concession of 1–9. Their average margin of victory during this period is a very impressive 8 points.

The Unbeaten Home Run

1997	Kerry	2–12	Tipperary	1–10	Austin Stack Park
1998	Kerry	1–14	Cork	1–11	Fitzgerald Stadium
1999	Kerry	1–11	Tipperary	0–8	Austin Stack Park
1999	Kerry	3–17	Clare	0–12	Fitzgerald Stadium
2000	Kerry	2–15	Cork	1–13	Fitzgerald Stadium
2001	Kerry	1–15	Limerick	0–10	Fitzgerald Stadium
2002	Kerry	0–8	Cork	0–8	Fitzgerald Stadium
2003	Kerry	0–25	Tipperary	1–10	Austin Stack Park
2003	Kerry	1–11	Limerick	0–9	Fitzgerald Stadium
2004	Kerry	0–15	Cork	0–7	Fitzgerald Stadium
2004	Kerry	3–10	Limerick	2–9	Fitzgerald Stadium

2006	Kerry	0–16	Waterford	0–8	Fitzgerald Stadium
2006	Kerry	0–17	Tipperary	1–5	Fitzgerald Stadium
2006	Kerry	0–10	Cork	0–10	Fitzgerald Stadium
2006	Kerry	4–11	Longford	1–11	Fitzgerald Stadium
2007	Kerry	1–15	Cork	1–13	Fitzgerald Stadium
2008	Kerry	1–14	Clare	0–5	Fitzgerald Stadium
2009	Kerry	0–13	Cork	1–10	Fitzgerald Stadium
2009	Kerry	0–14	Sligo	1–10	Austin Stack Park
2010	Kerry	0–15	Cork	0–15	Fitzgerald Stadium
2010	Kerry	1–17	Limerick	1–14	Fitzgerald Stadium
2011	Kerry	2–16	Tipperary	0–11	Fitzgerald Stadium
2011	Kerry	1–15	Cork	1–12	Fitzgerald Stadium

2012	Kerry	1–16	Tyrone	1–6	Fitzgerald Stadium
2013	Kerry	2–19	Tipperary	0–8	Fitzgerald Stadium
2013	Kerry	4–21	Waterford	1–4	Fitzgerald Stadium
2013	Kerry	1–16	Cork	0–17	Fitzgerald Stadium
2015	Kerry	2–15	Cork	3–12	Fitzgerald Stadium
2015	Kerry	1–11	Cork	1–6	Fitzgerald Stadium
2016	Kerry	2–23	Clare	0–17	Fitzgerald Stadium
2016	Kerry	3–17	Tipperary	2–10	Fitzgerald Stadium
2017	Kerry	1–23	Cork	0–15	Fitzgerald Stadium
2018	Kerry	0–32	Clare	0–10	Fitzgerald Stadium
2018	Kerry	3–25	Kildare	2–16	Fitzgerald Stadium

KINGPINS OF JUNIOR INTER-COUNTY FOOTBALL

The All-Ireland Junior Football Championship was first played in 1912 and has since been dominated by Munster's great rivals, Kerry and Cork.

Kerry are ahead in the overall pecking order with 19 titles, thanks to a wonderful recent run that saw the Kingdom win an unprecedented 4-in-a-row from 2015 to 2018. Cork are next in line with 17 titles. Kerry and Cork have won 7 of the All-Ireland titles on offer in this decade alone.

Stephen Wallace was the man in charge for the opening 2 titles in this recent 4-in-a-row success. Brosna's Jimmy Keane will be looking to win his third All-Ireland title and his county's 5th-in-a-row in 2019.

There has been talk in recent years of scrapping this competition, but it has proven to be a great recruitment ground for the Kerry Senior Football panel of late, with current Senior panellists like Shane Murphy, Jason Foley, Tadhg Morley, Gavin Crowley, Adrian Spillane, Killian Spillane, Tomás

Ó Sé and Graham O'Sullivan all winning All-Ireland Junior medals in recent years.

All-Ireland Junior Football Championship Roll of Honour

Kerry	(19)	1913, 1915, 1924, 1928, 1930, 1941, 1949, 1954, 1963, 1967, 1983, 1991, 1994, 2006, 2012, 2015, 2016, 2017, 2018
Cork	(17)	1951, 1953, 1955, 1964, 1972, 1984, 1987, 1989, 1990, 1993, 1996, 2001, 2005, 2007, 2009, 2011, 2013
London	(6)	1938, 1966, 1969, 1970, 1971, 1986
Dublin	(6)	1914, 1916, 1939, 1948, 1960, 2008
Mayo	(5)	1933, 1950, 1957, 1995, 1997
Meath	(5)	1947, 1952, 1962, 1988, 2003

Kerry's 19 Junior All-Ireland-Winning Teams

1913   Kerry 0–7   Carlow 1–2

A. Callaghan, J. Collins, J. Connell, J. Courtney, M. Daly, P. Foley, J. Keating, J. Kennedy, E. Hogan, P. O'Donnell, T. King, H. Murphy, E. Murphy, J. McCarthy, J. McGaley

1915   Kerry 0–6   Westmeath 1–2

J. Cronin, M. Carroll, J. Connor, M. Daly, J. Dunne, T. Doherty, B. Hickey, T. King, M. Moriarty, J. McGaley, R. Power, B. Sheehan, P. Slattery, P. Sullivan, J. Walsh

1924   Kerry 1–6   Longford 0–4

J. Riordan, P. Clifford, E. Fitzgerald, M. Graham, T. Graham, S. Kerins, T. Mahony, J. McCarthy, D. O'Connell, D. O'Connor, T. O'Connor, T. O'Donnell, W. Riordan, J. Slattery, P. Sullivan

1928   Kerry 2–8   Louth 2–3

T. Barrett, R. Clifford, T. Curran, M. Doyle, M. Healy, J. Horan, T. Landers, J. Murphy, B. McSweeney, T. O'Donnell, R. O'Donoghue, J. Price, J. Quill, R. Savage, J. Sullivan

1930   Kerry 2–2   Dublin 1–4

D. O'Keeffe, J. Flavin, C. Geaney, M. Healy, T. Landers, S. Moynihan, P. Murphy, J. O'Connor, J. O'Connor, D. O'Donoghue, M. O'Regan, L. Powell, J. Price, W. Quill, D. Spring

1941   Kerry 0–9   Cavan 0–4

J. Sheehy, T. Brosnan, T. O'Sullivan, T. Long, T. Barrett,

D. Lyne, T. Lyne, J. Sexton, J. Murphy, M. McCarthy, D. Healy, J. Kennington, W. O'Donnell, P. Donohue, P. McCarthy

1949   Kerry 2–14   Lancashire 0–6

L. Fitzgerald, J. O'Connor, T. Flynn, D. Dowling, M. Lynch, P. Shanahan, M. McElligott, S. Murphy, J. Dowling, P. Murphy, P. McCarthy, T. Long, J. Cooper, M. Palmer, J. Kennedy

1954   Kerry 1–7   London 1–5

N. Hussey, T. Spillane, J. O'Connor, T. Healy, T. Costelloe, J. Spillane, D. Falvey, E. Fitzgerald, D. Dillon, J. Culloty, T. Collins, S. Lovett, P. Fitzgerald, E. Dowling, B. Galvin

1963   Kerry 3–5   Lancashire 2–5

Tony Guerin, P. Kerins, Jack Dowling, Paddy Sayers, Tim Sheehan, Mick Morris, Joe O'Driscoll, Jer O'Connor, D. O'Sullivan, Tomo Burke, Brian Sheehy, Derry O'Shea, Teddy O'Dowd, John Burke, Dom O'Donnell

1967   Kerry 0–9   London 0–4

Weeshie Fogarty, Declan Lovett, D. O'Sullivan, G.

McCarthy, Derry Crowley, Mick Gleeson, Pat Ahern, M. O'Shea, Mick Ahern, P. O'Connor, Pat O'Connell, Willie Doran, Paudie Finnegan, Bill Kennedy, P. J. McIntyre. Sub: Bill McCarthy

1983   Kerry 0–15   Yorkshire 0–2

J. Kennelly, M. Colgan, Bernard O'Sullivan, Padraig Brosnan, Paudie Sheehan, Donie Hartnett, J. Stack, Ger O'Driscoll, Tom O'Connell, Jackie Walsh, R. O'Donoghue, P. O'Mahony, Johnny Doyle, Jerry O'Sullivan, Pat Sheehan. Subs: Gabriel Casey, Denis Higgins

1991   Kerry 2–14   London 0–5

Kieran Moran, T. Hanafin, Liam Burns, Tim Dennehy, Robbie O'Dwyer, Vincent Knightley, Packie Dillane, Fintan Ashe, Teddy Harrington, Denis Moynihan, Ger O'Driscoll, John Kennedy, Michael McAuliffe, Timmy Brosnan, Sean O'Sullivan. Subs: Shane Tuohy, Joe Murphy, Tom Evans

1994   Kerry 0–15   Galway 0–4

Declan O'Keeffe, Peter Lenihan, Liam Burns, John B. O'Brien, Jerome Stack, Kieran Scanlon, Stephen Stack, Donal Daly, Dara Ó Cinnéide, John Crowley, Michael

Keating, Denis Moynihan, Seamus Murphy, Seamus Fitzgerald, Paud O'Donoghue. Subs: Joe Daly, John Walsh, Conor O'Donnell

2006   Kerry 1–9   Roscommon 0–10

Sean Óg Ó Ciardubháin, Sean Hegarty, James Costello, Daniel Doyle, Denis O'Sullivan, Bryan Hickey, Jeremy King, John Paul Brosnan, Andrew Garnett, Niall Fleming, Michael Murphy, Conor Daly, Ronan McAuliffe, Stephen Wallace, John Buckley. Subs: Kieran Foley, Flor O'Sullivan, Fergal Griffin

2012   Kerry 0–19   Mayo 1–7

Sean Óg Ó Ciardubháin, Kieran Quirke, Brendan O'Mahony, Kevin O'Dwyer, Marcus Mangan, Jack Sherwood, James Walsh, Andrew Garnett, Alan O'Sullivan (0–1), Niall O'Mahony (0–5), Niall Ó Sé, Paul O'Donoghue, David O'Callaghan (0–3), Mike O'Donoghue (0–1), Conor Cox (0–8). Subs: Pat Corridan for Marcus Mangan, Michael Brennan for Andrew Garnett, Brendan Poff for Paul O'Donoghue, Colm Kerins (0–1) for David O'Callaghan, Eamonn Hickson for Kieran Quirke

2015   Kerry 2–18   Mayo 0–10

Shane Murphy, Dan O'Donoghue (0–1), Jack McGuire, David Culhane, James Walsh (0–1), Tadgh Morley (0–1), Gavin Crowley, Brendan O'Sullivan, Liam Kearney, Brian Crowley (0–1), Killian Spillane (0–2), Philip O'Connor (0–1), Thomas Hickey (2–4), Conor Cox (0–2), Alan O'Donoghue (0–4). Subs: Brian Sugrue for Jack McGuire, Eamon Kiely for Liam Kearney, David Griffin for Brian Crowley, Gary O'Sullivan for Killian Spillane, Michael Brennan for Gary O'Sullivan, Jeff O'Donoghue (0–1) for Conor Cox

2016   Kerry 2–18   Mayo 2–11

Darragh O'Shea, Fionán Clifford, Jason Foley (0-1), Cathal Ó Lúing, Patrick Clifford, Andrew Barry (0–1), Robert Wharton, Adrian Spillane (0–1), John C. O'Connor, Brian Ó Seanacháin, Paul O'Donoghue (0–3), David Foran (0–3), Niall Ó Sé (2–0), Kieran Hurley (0–3), Seán Michéal Ó Conchúir (0–5). Subs: Michael O'Donnell for Adrian Spillane, Dara O'Shea for Brian Ó Seanacháin, Dara Roche (0–1) for Kieran Hurley

2017   Kerry 2–19   Meath 1–14

Tomás Mac an tSaoir, Eamon Kiely, Jack McGuire, Brian Sugrue, James Walsh, Pa Kilkenny (0–1), Daniel

O'Brien, Roibeard Ó Sé, Brendan O'Sullivan, Philip O'Connor (0–3), Jeff O'Donoghue, Éanna Ó Conchúir (0–1), Killian Spillane (0–3), Conor Cox (1–8), Tomás Ó Sé (1–2). Subs: D. J. Murphy for Eamon Kiely, P. J. MacLaimh for James Walsh, Michael Foley for Pa Kilkenny, Ivan Parker (0–1) for Brendan O'Sullivan, Liam Carey for Jeff O'Donoghue, Stephen O'Sullivan for Conor Cox

2018   Kerry 2–13   Galway 2–11

Darragh O'Shea, Trevor Wallace, Dan O'Donoghue, Paul O'Sullivan, Pádraig O'Connor, Andrew Barry, Seán Moloney, Kieran Murphy, Ronan Murphy, Evan Cronin (0–2), Paudie Clifford (1–0), Denis Daly (0–1), Thomas Hickey (0–4), Lee O'Donoghue (0–2), Niall Ó Sé (1–4). Subs: Cillian Fitzgerald for Ronan Murphy, Ronan Buckley for Lee O'Donoghue, Conor O'Shea for Pádraig O'Connor (57)

2018 KERRY SENIOR INTER-COUNTY FOOTBALL PLAYER RECORDS

Eamonn Fitzmaurice used 28 players in the 2018 championship and 37 in the National League. Listed below are the players who played Senior championship football and League football in 2018 with their full championship appearances and scoring records, as well as League appearances and scoring records.

Kieran Donaghy, Anthony Maher, Darran O'Sullivan and Donnchadh Walsh have all since retired from Senior inter-county football. Shane Enright missed the entire championship through injury. He had previously made 33 championship appearances and scored 0–2, and will no doubt hope to be part of Kerry's championship charge in 2019.

League Appearances

Shane Murphy	Apps: 5	Scored: 0–1
Jason Foley	Apps: 9	
Tadhg Morley	Apps: 9	Scored: 0–2

Shane Enright   Apps: 48   Scored: 0–1

Paul Murphy   Apps: 36   Scored: 0–18

Peter Crowley   Apps: 45   Scored: 1–12

David Moran   Apps: 51   Scored: 3–39

Jack Barry   Apps: 13   Scored: 0–5

Micheál Burns   Apps: 7   Scored: 0–9

Sean O'Shea   Apps: 5   Scored: 0–20

Stephen O'Brien   Apps: 33   Scored: 3–28

David Clifford   Apps: 6   Scored: 0–21

Paul Geaney   Apps: 28   Scored: 10–74

James O'Donoghue   Apps: 25   Scored: 7–44

Brian Kelly   Apps: 16

Tom O'Sullivan   Apps: 7   Scored: 0–2

Kevin McCarthy   Apps: 9   Scored: 0–6

Barry John Keane   Apps: 51   Scored: 2–79

Mikey Geaney   Apps: 23   Scored: 1–8

Barry O'Sullivan   Apps: 8   Scored: 0–1

Ronan Shanahan   Apps: 13   Scored: 0–1

Mark Griffin	Apps: 36	Scored: 0–1
Gavin Crowley	Apps: 4	Scored: 1–1
Brian Ó Beaglaíoch	Apps: 7	
Fionn Fitzgerald	Apps: 28	Scored: 0–1
Jack Savage	Apps: 9	Scored: 0–7
Killian Young	Apps: 53	Scored: 0–2
Brendan O'Sullivan	Apps: 14	Scored: 0–8
Adrian Spillane	Apps: 7	
Daithí Casey	Apps: 13	Scored: 0–9
Éanna Ó Conchúir	Apps: 5	
Cormac Coffey	Apps: 3	Scored: 0–1
Killian Spillane	Apps: 4	Scored: 0–6
Matthew Flaherty	Apps: 5	Scored: 0–1
Andrew Barry	Apps: 2	
Brian Ó Seanacháin	Apps: 2	
Greg Horan	Apps: 1	

Championship Appearances

Brian Kelly	Apps: 17	
Shane Murphy	Apps: 3	Scored: 0–1
Jason Foley	Apps: 4	
Peter Crowley	Apps: 33	Scored: 0–3
Tom O'Sullivan	Apps: 4	Scored: 0–2
Paul Murphy	Apps: 25	Scored: 2–12
Killian Young	Apps: 62	Scored: 0–7
Gavin White	Apps: 5	Scored: 0–1
David Moran	Apps: 36	Scored: 1–13
Jack Barry	Apps: 10	Scored: 0–5
Micheál Burns	Apps: 4	Scored: 0–4
Sean O'Shea	Apps: 5	Scored: 0–24
Stephen O'Brien	Apps: 24	Scored: 5–31
David Clifford	Apps: 5	Scored: 4–18
Paul Geaney	Apps: 27	Scored: 9–94
Kevin McCarthy	Apps: 6	Scored: 0–2

James O'Donoghue	Apps: 37	Scored: 10–103
Darran O'Sullivan	Apps: 70	Scored: 11–38
Tadhg Morley	Apps: 12	Scored: 0–1
Brian Ó Beaglaíoch	Apps: 9	
Ronan Shanahan	Apps: 2	
Mark Griffin	Apps: 18	
Fionn Fitzgerald	Apps: 19	Scored: 0–4
Barry John Keane	Apps: 37	Scored: 2–37
Mikey Geaney	Apps: 15	Scored: 0–9
Kieran Donaghy	Apps: 69	Scored: 14–69
Donnchadh Walsh	Apps: 53	Scored: 5–25
Anthony Maher	Apps: 45	Scored: 1–17

KERRY'S 37 ALL-IRELAND SENIOR FOOTBALL WINNING TEAMS

1903 (17-a-side): Kerry vs London in Jones Road on 12 November 1905. Score: Kerry 0–11 London 0–3

Denny Breen, John Buckley, Denny Curran, Paddy Dillon, Dick Fitzgerald, John Fitzgerald, Con Healy, Roddy Kirwan, Denny Kissane, Billy Lynch, Dan McCarthy, Maurice McCarthy, Jack Myers, Jamesie O'Gorman, Thady O'Gorman, Florrie O'Sullivan, Austin Stack

1904: Kerry vs Dublin in Cork on 1 July 1906. Score: Kerry 0–5 Dublin 0–2

Denny Breen, John Buckley, P. J. Cahill, Denny Curran, Paddy Dillon, Dick Fitzgerald, John T. Fitzgerald, Con Healy, Billy Lynch, Dan McCarthy, Maurice McCarthy, Jack Myers, Jamesie O'Gorman, Thady O'Gorman, Florrie O'Sullivan, John O'Sullivan, Austin Stack

1909: Kerry vs Louth in Jones Road on 5 December 1909. Score: Kerry 1–9 Louth 0–6

Denny Breen, Tom Costelloe, Frank Cronin, Paddy Dillon, Dick Fitzgerald, Con Healy, Paddy Kenneally,

Maurice McCarthy, John McCarthy, Paddy Mullane, Con Murphy, Batt O'Connor, John O'Sullivan, Michael Quinlan, Tom Rice, Johnny Skinner, Ned Spillane

1913 (15-a-side): Kerry vs Wexford in Croke Park on 14 December 1913. Score: Kerry 2–2 Wexford 0–3

Danny Mullins, Con Clifford, Tom Costelloe, Denis Doyle, Dick Fitzgerald, Paddy Healy, Paddy Kenneally, Jack Lawlor, Maurice McCarthy, Con Murphy, John O'Mahony, Pat O'Shea, Jack Rice, Tom Rice, Johnny Skinner

1914: Kerry vs Wexford in Croke Park on 29 November 1914 (replay). Score: Kerry 2–3 Wexford 0–6

Danny Mullins, P. Breen, Con Clifford, Tom Costelloe, Denis Doyle, Dick Fitzgerald, Paddy Healy, Jack Lawlor, Maurice McCarthy, Con Murphy, John O'Mahony, Pat O'Shea, Jack Rice, Tom Rice, Johnny Skinner

1924: Kerry vs Dublin in Croke Park on 26 April 1924. Score: Kerry 0–4 Dublin 0–3

John Sheehy, Jas Bailey, John Bailey, Joe Barrett, Con Brosnan, Bill Landers, Jerry Moriarty, John Murphy, R. Prenderville, Paul Russell, Jackie Ryan, John Joe Sheehy, Bob Stack, Phil Sullivan, Jack Walsh

1926: Kerry vs Kildare in Croke Park on 17 October 1926 (replay). Score: Kerry 1–4 Kildare 0–4

Johnny Riordan, Jas Bailey, Joe Barrett, Con Brosnan, Pat Clifford, William O'Gorman, Tom Mahoney, Jerry Moriarty, Denis O'Connell, Paul Russell, Jackie Ryan, John Joe Sheehy, John Slattery, Bob Stack, Jack Walsh

1929: Kerry vs Kildare in Croke Park on 22 September 1929. Score: Kerry 1–8 Kildare 1–5

Johnny Riordan, Dee O'Connor, Joe Barrett, Jack Walsh, Paul Russell, Joe O'Sullivan, Tim O'Donnell, Con Brosnan, Bob Stack, Jackie Ryan (0–1), Miko Doyle, John Joe Landers (0–1), Ned Sweeney (1–0), Jas Bailey, John Joe Sheehy (0–6)

1930: Kerry vs Monaghan in Croke Park on 28 September 1930. Score: Kerry 3–11 Monaghan 0–2

Johnny Riordan, Dee O'Connor, Joe Barrett, Jack Walsh, Paul Russell, Joe O'Sullivan, Tim O'Donnell, Con Brosnan, Bob Stack, Jackie Ryan (0–3), Miko Doyle (0–2), Eamonn Fitzgerald, Ned Sweeney (1–0), John Joe Landers (2–3), John Joe Sheehy (0–3)

1931: Kerry vs Kildare in Croke Park on 27 September 1931. Score: Kerry 1–11 Kildare 0–8

Dan O'Keeffe, Dee O'Connor, Joe Barrett, Jack Walsh,

Paul Russell (1–0), Joe O'Sullivan, Tim Landers, Con Brosnan, Bob Stack, John Joe Landers (0–2), Miko Doyle (0–1), Eamonn Fitzgerald, Jackie Ryan (0–6), Paddy Whitty (0–2), Martin O'Regan

1932: Kerry vs Mayo in Croke Park on 25 September 1932. Score: Kerry 2–7 Mayo 2–4

Dan O'Keeffe, Dee O'Connor, Joe Barrett, Jack Walsh, Paul Russell, Joe O'Sullivan, Paddy Whitty, Bob Stack, Johnny Walsh, Con Geaney, Miko Doyle (1–1), Tim Landers (1–1), Jackie Ryan (0–4), Con Brosnan (0–1), John Joe Landers

1937: Kerry vs Cavan in Croke Park on 17 October 1937 (replay). Score: Kerry 4–4 Cavan 1–7

Dan O'Keeffe, Bill Kinnerk, Joe Keohane, Bill Myers, Tim O'Donnell, Bill Dillon, Tadhg Healy, Johnny Walsh, Sean Brosnan, Jack Flavin, Charlie O'Sullivan, Tim Landers (0–4), John Joe Landers (1–0), Miko Doyle (1–0), Tim O'Leary (2–0). Sub: Tom 'Gega' O'Connor

1939: Kerry vs Meath in Croke Park on 24 September 1939. Score: Kerry 2–5 Meath 2–3

Dan O'Keeffe, Bill Myers, Joe Keohane, Tadhg Healy, Bill Dillon, Bill Casey, Eddie Walsh, Paddy Kennedy, Jimmy 'Gawksie' O'Gorman, Murt Kelly (0–2), Tom 'Gega' O'Connor, Johnny Walsh (0–1), Charlie O'Sullivan, Dan Spring (2–1), Tim Landers (0–1)

1940: Kerry vs Galway in Croke Park on 22 September 1940. Score: Kerry 0–7 Galway 1–3

Dan O'Keeffe, Bill Myers, Joe Keohane, Tadhg Healy, Bill Dillon, Bill Casey, Eddie Walsh, Sean Brosnan, Johnny Walsh, Jimmy 'Gawksie' O'Gorman, Tom 'Gega' O'Connor (0–1), Paddy Kennedy, Murt Kelly (0–2), Dan Spring (0–1), Charlie O'Sullivan (0–2). Sub: Paddy 'Bawn' Brosnan (0–1)

1941: Kerry vs Galway in Croke Park on 7 September 1941. Score: Kerry 1–8 Galway 0–7

Dan O'Keeffe, Bill Myers, Joe Keohane, Tadhg Healy, Bill Dillon, Bill Casey, Eddie Walsh, Sean Brosnan, Paddy Kennedy, Johnny Walsh, Tom 'Gega' O'Connor (1–1), Paddy 'Bawn' Brosnan (0–2), Jimmy 'Gawksie' O'Gorman (0–3), Murt Kelly (0–2), Charlie O'Sullivan. Subs: Tim Landers, Mikey Lyne

1946: Kerry vs Roscommon in Croke Park on 27 October 1946 (replay). Score: Kerry 2–8 Roscommon 0–10

Dan O'Keeffe, Dinny Lyne, Joe Keohane, Paddy 'Bawn' Brosnan, Jackie Lyne, Bill Casey, Eddie Walsh, Paddy Kennedy (0–1), Teddy O'Connor, Jackie Falvey, Tom 'Gega' O'Connor (1–4), Batt Garvey (0–2), Frank O'Keeffe, Paddy Burke (1–0), Dan Kavanagh. Sub: Gus Cremin (0–1)

1953: Kerry vs Armagh in Croke Park on 27 September 1953. Score: Kerry 0–13 Armagh 1–6

Johnny Foley, Jas Murphy, Ned Roche, Donie Murphy, Colm Kennelly, John Cronin, 'Micksie' Palmer, Seán Murphy, Dermot Hanifin, Jim Brosnan (0–4), John Joe Sheehan (0–3), Tadhgie Lyne (0–4), Tom Ashe (0–1), Sean Kelly, Jackie Lyne (0–1). Sub: Gerald O'Sullivan

1955: Kerry vs Dublin in Croke Park on 25 September 1955. Score: Kerry 0–12 Dublin 1–6

Gary O'Mahony, Jerome O'Shea, Ned Roche, 'Micksie' Palmer, Seán Murphy, John Cronin, Tom Moriarty, John Dowling (0–1), Dinny O'Shea, Paudie Sheehy (0–1), Tom Costelloe, Tadhgie Lyne (0–6), Johnny Culloty, Mick Murphy (0–1), Jim Brosnan (0–2). Sub: John Joe Sheehan (0–1)

1959: Kerry vs Galway in Croke Park on 27 September 1959. Score: Kerry 3–7 Galway 1–4

Johnny Culloty, Jerome O'Shea, Niall Sheehy, Tim Lyons, Seán Murphy, Kevin Coffey, Mick O'Dwyer (0–1), Mick O'Connell, Seamus Murphy, Dan McAuliffe (2–2), Tom Long, Paudie Sheehy, Dave Geaney, John Dowling (0–2), Tadhgie Lyne (0–2). Subs: Jack Dowling, Maurice O'Connell, Gary McMahon (1–0)

1962: Kerry vs Roscommon in Croke Park on 23 September 1962. Score: Kerry 1–12 Roscommon 1–6

Johnny Culloty, Seamus Murphy, Niall Sheehy, Tim Lyons, Sean Óg Sheehy, Noel Lucey, Mick O'Dwyer, Mick O'Connell (0–8), Jimmy Lucey, Dan McAuliffe, Timmy O'Sullivan (0–2), Jerry O'Riordan, Gary Mc-Mahon (1–0), Tom Long, Paudie Sheehy (0–2). Subs: J. J. Barrett, Kevin Coffey

1969: Kerry vs Offaly in Croke Park on 28 September 1969. Score: Kerry 0–10 Offaly 0–7

Johnny Culloty, Seamus Murphy, Paud O'Donoghue, Seamus Fitzgerald, Tom Prendergast, Mick Morris, Micheál O'Shea, Mick O'Connell (0–2), D. J. Crowley (0–2), Brendan Lynch (0–1), Pat Griffin, Eamonn O'Donoghue, Mick Gleeson (0–2), Liam Higgins (0–1), Mick O'Dwyer (0–2)

1970: Kerry vs Meath in Croke Park on 27 September 1970. Score: Kerry 2–19 Meath 0–18

Johnny Culloty, Seamus Murphy, Paud O'Donoghue, Donie O'Sullivan, Tom Prendergast, John O'Keeffe, Micheál O'Shea, Mick O'Connell (0–2), D. J. Crowley (1–0), Brendan Lynch (0–6), Pat Griffin (0–2), Eamonn O'Donoghue (0–2), Mick Gleeson (1–1), Liam Higgins (0–2), Mick O'Dwyer (0–4). Sub: Seamus Fitzgerald

1975: Kerry vs Dublin in Croke Park on 28 September 1975. Score: Kerry 2–12 Dublin 0–11

Paudie O'Mahoney, Ger O'Keeffe, John O'Keeffe, Jimmy Deenihan, Páidí Ó Sé, Tim Kennelly, Ger Power, Paudie Lynch, Pat McCarthy, Brendan Lynch (0–3), Denis 'Ogie' Moran (0–2), Mickey Ned O'Sullivan, John Egan (1–0), Mikey Sheehy (0–4), Pat Spillane (0–3). Sub: Ger O'Driscoll (1–0)

1978: Kerry vs Dublin in Croke Park on 24 September 1978. Score: Kerry 5–11 Dublin 0–9

Charlie Nelligan, Jimmy Deenihan, John O'Keeffe, Mick Spillane, Páidí Ó Sé, Tim Kennelly, Paudie Lynch, Jack O'Shea (0–1), Sean Walsh, Ger Power (0–1), Denis 'Ogie' Moran, Pat Spillane (0–1), Mikey Sheehy (1–4), Eoin Liston (3–2), John Egan (1–2). Sub: Paudie O'Mahoney

1979: Kerry vs Dublin in Croke Park on 16 September 1979. Score: Kerry 3–13 Dublin 1–8

Charlie Nelligan, Jimmy Deenihan, John O'Keeffe, Mick Spillane, Páidí Ó Sé, Tim Kennelly, Paudie Lynch, Jack O'Shea (0–1), Sean Walsh, Tommy Doyle, Denis 'Ogie' Moran, Pat Spillane (0–4), Mikey Sheehy (2–6), Eoin Liston (0–1), John Egan (1–1). Sub: Vincent O'Connor

1980: Kerry vs Roscommon in Croke Park on 21 September 1980. Score: Kerry 1–9 Roscommon 1–6

Charlie Nelligan, Jimmy Deenihan, John O'Keeffe, Paudie Lynch, Páidí Ó Sé, Tim Kennelly, Ger O'Keeffe, Jack O'Shea (0–1), Sean Walsh, Ger Power (0–1), Denis 'Ogie' Moran, Pat Spillane (0–1), Mikey Sheehy (1–6), Tommy Doyle, John Egan. Sub: Ger O'Driscoll

1981: Kerry vs Offaly in Croke Park on 20 September 1981. Score: Kerry 1–12 Offaly 0–8

Charlie Nelligan, Jimmy Deenihan, John O'Keeffe, Paudie Lynch, Páidí Ó Sé (0–1), Tim Kennelly, Mick Spillane, Jack O'Shea (1–0), Sean Walsh (0–1), Ger Power (0–2), Denis 'Ogie' Moran (0–1), Tommy Doyle (0–1), Mikey Sheehy (0–5), Eoin Liston, John Egan (0–1). Subs: Pat Spillane, Ger O'Keeffe

1984: Kerry vs Dublin in Croke Park on 23 September 1984. Score: Kerry 0–14 Dublin 1–6

Charlie Nelligan, Páidí Ó Sé, Sean Walsh, Mick Spillane, Tommy Doyle, Tom Spillane, Ger Lynch, Jack O'Shea (0–1), Ambrose O'Donovan, John Kennedy (0–5), Denis 'Ogie' Moran, Pat Spillane (0–4), Ger Power, Eoin Liston (0–3), John Egan. Sub: Timmy O'Dowd

1985: Kerry vs Dublin in Croke Park on 22 September 1985. Score: Kerry 2–12 Dublin 2–8

Charlie Nelligan, Páidí Ó Sé, Sean Walsh, Mick Spillane, Tommy Doyle (0–1), Tom Spillane, Ger Lynch, Jack O'Shea (1–3), Ambrose O'Donovan, Timmy O'Dowd (1–1), Denis 'Ogie' Moran (0–1), Pat Spillane (0–2), Mikey Sheehy (0–3), Eoin Liston, Ger Power. Sub: John Kennedy (0–1)

1986: Kerry vs Tyrone in Croke Park on 21 September 1986. Score: Kerry 2–15 Tyrone 1–10

Charlie Nelligan, Páidí Ó Sé, Sean Walsh, Mick Spillane, Tommy Doyle, Tom Spillane, Ger Lynch, Jack O'Shea, Ambrose O'Donovan, Willie Maher, Denis 'Ogie' Moran (0–2), Pat Spillane (1–4), Mikey Sheehy (1–4), Eoin Liston (0–2), Ger Power (0–1). Sub: Timmy O'Dowd (0–2)

1997: Kerry vs Mayo in Croke Park on 28 September 1997. Score: Kerry 0–13 Mayo 1–7

Declan O'Keeffe, Killian Burns, Barry O'Shea, Stephen Stack, Seamus Moynihan, Liam O'Flaherty, Eamonn Breen, Darragh Ó Sé (0–1), William Kirby, Pa Laide (0–2), Liam Hassett, Denis O'Dwyer, Billy O'Shea, Dara Ó Cinnéide, Maurice Fitzgerald (0–9). Subs: Johnny Crowley (0–1), Donal Daly, Mike Frank Russell

2000: Kerry vs Galway in Croke Park on 7 October 2000 (replay). Score: Kerry 0–17 Galway 1–10

Declan O'Keeffe, Mike Hassett, Seamus Moynihan, Mike McCarthy, Tomás Ó Sé, Eamonn Fitzmaurice (0–1), Tom O'Sullivan, Darragh Ó Sé, Donal Daly, Aodán Mac Gearailt (0–2), Liam Hassett (0–4), Noel Kennelly (0–1), Mike Frank Russell (0–2), Dara Ó Cinnéide (0–4), Johnny Crowley (0–3). Subs: Maurice Fitzgerald, Tommy Griffin

2004: Kerry vs Mayo in Croke Park on 26 September 2004. Score: Kerry 1–20 Mayo 2–9

Diarmuid Murphy, Tom O'Sullivan, Mike McCarthy, Aidan O'Mahony, Marc Ó Sé (0–1), Tomás Ó Sé, Eamonn Fitzmaurice, Eoin Brosnan, William Kirby (0–3), Liam Hassett, Darran O'Sullivan (0–1), Paul Galvin (0–1), Colm Cooper (1–5), Dara Ó Cinnéide (0–8), Johnny Crowley. Subs: Seamus Moynihan, Mike Frank Russell (0–1), Ronan O'Connor, Paddy Kelly, Brendan Guiney

2006: Kerry vs Mayo in Croke Park on 17 September 2006. Score: Kerry 4–15 Mayo 3–5

Diarmuid Murphy, Marc Ó Sé, Mike McCarthy, Tom O'Sullivan, Tomás Ó Sé, Seamus Moynihan (0–1), Aidan O'Mahony (0–2), Darragh Ó Sé, Tommy

Griffin, Sean O'Sullivan (0–1), Declan O'Sullivan (1–2), Paul Galvin (0–1), Colm Cooper (1–2), Kieran Donaghy (1–2), Mike Frank Russell (0–2). Subs: Eoin Brosnan (1–1), Darran O'Sullivan, Bryan Sheehan (0–1), Eamonn Fitzmaurice, Brendan Guiney

2007: Kerry vs Cork in Croke Park on 16 September 2007. Score: Kerry 3–13 Cork 1–9

Diarmuid Murphy, Marc Ó Sé, Tom O'Sullivan, Pádraig Reidy, Tomás Ó Sé (0–1), Aidan O'Mahony (0–1), Killian Young, Darragh Ó Sé, Seamus Scanlon (0–1), Paul Galvin (0–1), Declan O'Sullivan (0–1), Eoin Brosnan, Colm Cooper (1–5), Kieran Donaghy (2–0), Bryan Sheehan (0–2). Subs: Sean O'Sullivan (0–1), Darran O'Sullivan, Tommy Griffin, Mossie Lyons, Mike Frank Russell

2009: Kerry vs Cork in Croke Park on 20 September 2009. Score: Kerry 0–16 Cork 1–9

Diarmuid Murphy, Marc Ó Sé, Tommy Griffin, Tom O'Sullivan, Tomás Ó Sé (0–2), Mike McCarthy, Killian Young, Darragh Ó Sé, Seamus Scanlon, Paul Galvin, Declan O'Sullivan (0–1), Tadhg Kennelly (0–2), Colm Cooper (0–6), Tommy Walsh (0–4), Darran O'Sullivan (0–1). Subs: Donnchadh Walsh, Micheál Quirke, Kieran Donaghy, David Moran, Aidan O'Mahony

2014: Kerry vs Donegal in Croke Park on 21 September 2014. Score: Kerry 2–9 Donegal 0–12

Brian Kelly, Marc Ó Sé, Aidan O'Mahony, Fionn Fitzgerald, Paul Murphy (0–1), Peter Crowley, Killian Young, Anthony Maher, David Moran, Stephen O'Brien, Johnny Buckley (0–1), Donnchadh Walsh, Paul Geaney (1–2), Kieran Donaghy (1–2), James O'Donoghue. Subs: Mikey Geaney, Barry John Keane (0–2), Shane Enright, Darran O'Sullivan, Bryan Sheehan (0–1), Kieran O'Leary

5 Football Facts

1. Seamus Murphy (Camp) played in 11 Munster Senior Football finals and never tasted defeat in a final.

2. Kerry won the last 60-minute All-Ireland Senior Football final (1969), the first 80-minute final (1970) and the first 70-minute final (1975).

3. Seamus Murphy (St Pat's, Blennerville) won 2 All-Ireland Junior medals as a forward but started off his county career as a goalkeeper when Kerry won the Munster Minor Championship in 1989.

4. Mikey Sheehy was the only Kerry player not to miss a championship game from the Munster semi-final in 1975 to the All-Ireland semi-final in 1984. Injury prevented him from playing in the All-Ireland Centenary final.

5. Neilie Donovan played midfield for Kerry when they won the All-Ireland Minor final in 1975. Five years later, when Kerry again won the All-

Ireland Minor title, Neilie's brother Ambrose also lined out in midfield.

THE GREATEST
KERRY TEAMS

THE ORIGINAL OF THE SPECIES:
KERRY'S 4-IN-A-ROW WINNERS 1929–32

This was the original Kerry team of greats. Their record was phenomenal at the time, as they completed a 4-in-a-row of League and All-Ireland titles.

The trainer of the side was Jack McCarthy from Strand Road in Tralee and he assembled a team of strong but immensely gifted footballers. However, it was Kerry County Board Chairman Din Joe Bailey who was arguably the architect of the new-look Kerry side. The Ballymac man served as Kerry County Board Chairman from 1928 to 1952. Bailey managed to get the likes of Con Brosnan, Joe Barrett and John Joe Sheehy to put their political differences to one side for the greater good of the County Kerry football team and the rest, as they say, is history.

It all started with a win over Kildare in the All-Ireland final of 1929. A second All-Ireland win followed in 1930 as Kerry cruised to victory over Monaghan with the great John Joe 'Purty' Landers the star of the show, scoring 2–3 in that game.

The 3-in-a-row was completed in 1931 when

Kerry defeated Kildare in the final for the second time in 3 years. Jackie Ryan scored 6 points in that final win, while wing back Paul Russell scored the only goal of the game. It turns out they had attacking wing backs in the 1930s as well!

That year Dan O'Keeffe and Martin 'Bracker' O'Regan came into the side in goal and at corner forward respectively. Both would go on to become Kerry football legends in their own right.

Kerry travelled to America in 1931 and beat every team that they played. Inspired by their foreign travels, the Kerry men stormed to victory and their 4-in-a-row with a 3-point win over Mayo in 1932.

The names of the men involved will forever be etched in the folklore of Kerry football.

The Finals

1929 22 September
Kerry 1–8   Kildare 1–5   Croke Park   43,839

1930 28 September
Kerry 3–11   Monaghan 0–2   Croke Park   33,280

1931 27 September
Kerry 1–11   Kildare 0–8   Croke Park   42,350

1932 25 September
Kerry 2–7   Mayo 2–4   Croke Park   25,816

MICKO'S BACHELORS

This Kerry side is considered one of the greatest, if not the greatest, to ever play the game. Micko's 'Team of Bachelors' broke record after record and won 8 All-Ireland Senior Football titles in 12 years. It all started in 1974 when Mick O'Dwyer, the former inter-county player from Waterville, took over as team manager. Immediately he brought in a number of new and talented players, who fused smoothly with a solid group that had all come on board in the previous few years.

In 1975 Kerry shocked the GAA world with a glorious win over Kevin Heffernan's previously all-conquering Dublin side in the All-Ireland final on a scoreline of 2–12 to 0–11. That started a rivalry that to this day is considered to be the greatest the game has ever seen.

Maybe the win was slightly premature, however, in terms of declaring Kerry as the dominant team, as Dublin came back with All-Ireland wins in 1976 and 1977. Hard as it is to believe now, O'Dwyer very nearly lost his job following the 1977 loss, but the coach and his 'bachelors' came roaring back in

1978 in that never-to-be-forgotten All-Ireland win over Dublin.

This was the year when the great Kerry team really fell into place. The final featured a 'Bomber' Liston hat-trick of goals and the infamous Mikey Sheehy chipped goal over a despairing Paddy Cullen. It was gloriously described as the 'Sheeky' goal. Kerry ultimately defeated Dublin by 5–11 to 0–9 in that final, despite the fact that Dublin had led by 0–6 to 0–1 after twenty minutes.

In 1979 Kerry reigned supreme once more, as an aging Dublin side were no match for a Kerry team inspired by Mikey Sheehy. Sheehy's total of 2–6 in the final was a record, equalling Dublin player Jimmy Keaveney's total of 2–6 from the All-Ireland final of 1977 against Armagh. These aggregate scores of 12 points remain the most scored by any individual in a Senior All-Ireland final.

Wins over Roscommon and Offaly in 1980 and 1981 completed a 4-in-a-row, meaning that this Kerry side joined the Kerry team of 1929–32 and Wexford's team of 1915–18 as the only sides in the game to win a 4-in-a-row of All-Ireland Senior Football titles (until Dublin joined that elite group in 2018).

1982 will go down in history as the year that Kerry lost the All-Ireland final and their chance to win an historic 5-in-a-row when Offaly's Seamus Darby scored a late goal. Another sucker-punch followed in 1983 when a late Tadhg Murphy goal saw Cork take the Munster title.

Few would have believed that this great group of Kerry warriors would come back from such disappointments, but they did.

Micko inspired his team to win the Centenary All-Ireland final in 1984 and once again it was Dublin's crown that they took. A new breed had emerged by that stage, with captain Ambrose O'Donovan, Ger Lynch, Tom Spillane, John Kennedy, Timmy O'Dowd and Willie Maher all driving the team forward alongside the established greats.

This Kerry team subsequently went on to win a 3-in-a-row to add to their previous 4-in-a-row and by the end of this unprecedented run few could deny that this was the greatest football team of all time.

Five men from that era hold the record for the most Senior All-Ireland football titles won – Pat Spillane, Páidí Ó Sé, Ogie Moran, Mikey Sheehy and Ger Power all winning 8 medals. Spillane also won a record 9 football All Stars.

The 'Golden Years' video, which documented this team's unparalleled success, sold widely across Kerry on its release. It had a musical backdrop of the James Bond theme song 'Nobody Does it Better' – a perfect tune to sum up the greatest era in the history of Kerry football.

Kerry's 8 All-Ireland Senior Titles 1975–86

1975 28 September
Kerry 2–12   Dublin 0–11   Croke Park   66,346

1978 24 September
Kerry 5–11   Dublin 0–9   Croke Park   71,503

1979 16 September
Kerry 3–13   Dublin 1–8   Croke Park   72,185

1980 21 September
Kerry 1–9   Roscommon 1–6 Croke Park   63,854

1981 20 September
Kerry 1–12   Offaly 0–8   Croke Park   61,489

1984 23 September
Kerry 0–14   Dublin 1–6   Croke Park   68,365

1985 22 September
Kerry 2–12   Dublin 2–8   Croke Park   69,389

1986 21 September
Kerry 2–15   Tyrone 1–10   Croke Park   68,628

LADIES' 9-IN-A-ROW SIDE

While the men's team had a disastrous end to 1982, that year was the beginning of another glorious chapter in Kerry football.

The ladies game was in its infancy with the first Senior Ladies All-Ireland final played in 1974. Kerry won their first All-Ireland title in 1976 when they defeated Offaly by 4–6 to 1–5 at Littleton GAA pitch in Tipperary.

When Kerry won their second title, in 1982, the game was played against, of all counties, Offaly! That they won was some small consolation for Kerry folk. What followed, however, was barely believable, as Kerry went on to win 9 All-Ireland Ladies titles in a row from 1982 to 1990.

In 1986 Kerry played the first Ladies final in Croke Park when they defeated Wexford. This was of course also their 5-in-a-row. There were great scenes of joy in Croke Park as the Kerry Ladies managed to go one better than their male counterparts. That was only the beginning, however, as they went on to win 4 more consecutive titles, all in Croke Park.

That Kerry team featured many players who became household names, none more so than Mary Jo Curran, who won a record 11 All Stars. (This record was equalled by Mayo's Cora Staunton in 2017.) Mary Jo's sister, Phil, and namesake Kathleen, also starred in that team, as did the Lawlor sisters, Margaret and Eileen, from Ardfert. There were other great names in that side too, like Del Whyte, Bridget Leen, Marina Barry and Annette Walsh.

The trainer largely responsible for this great period of success was Mick Fitzgerald. Fitzgerald received a GAA President's Award for his contribution to Ladies football in 2008. Mick was at the original meeting of the new Ladies Board in Hayes' Hotel in 1974 and he later became President of the Ladies Football Association (1982–85). He was also a selector and manager on different occasions in all of Kerry's All-Ireland triumphs at Senior level, and was involved from start to finish as trainer of the great Kerry 9-in-a-row-winning team.

Speaking before he received the President's Award, Fitzgerald recounted the humble beginnings of Ladies football. 'I remember organising one of the first Ladies games of football back in 1973. Kerry played Cork at a carnival in Banteer and around 1,500 hundred people showed up for the novelty value of watching Ladies football. When we set the Association up back in 1974 we never thought that the game would grow like it has. It has exceeded my expectations and I am immensely proud of the Association.'

Kerry's 9 All-Ireland Final Wins

1982

| Kerry 1–8 | Offaly 1–2 | MacDonagh Park, Nenagh |

1983

| Kerry 4–6 | Wexford 1–7 | Kilsheelan, Tipperary |

1984

| Kerry 0–5 | Leitrim 0–3 | Páirc Mochua, Timahoe |

1985

| Kerry 2–9 | Laois 0–5 | Páirc Uí Chaoimh, Cork |

1986

| Kerry 1–11 | Wexford 0–8 | Croke Park, Dublin |

1987

| Kerry 2–10 | Westmeath 2–2 | Croke Park, Dublin |

1988

| Kerry 2–12 | Laois 3–3 | Croke Park, Dublin |

1989

| Kerry 1–14 | Wexford 1–5 | Croke Park, Dublin |

1990

| Kerry 1–9 | Laois 0–6 | Croke Park, Dublin |

THE GOLDEN YEARS 2:
2004–09

In this era Kerry appeared in 6 All-Ireland finals in a row, winning 4 in 2004, 2006–07 and 2009. Kerry lost finals to Tyrone in 2005 and 2008, but few could ever doubt the brilliance of the teams from this time. The 2004–09 squads will surely be judged as some of the greatest to have played the game.

Jack O'Connor came in as manager in 2004, taking over from Páidí Ó Sé, and he quickly set about changing the face of the side. The introduction of players like Paul Galvin and Aidan O'Mahony, for example, was crucial to its subtle evolution. This duo added a bit of badly needed bite to the Kerry side.

Northern teams Tyrone and Armagh had won the previous 2 All-Ireland titles with quite a tenacious and defensive style of play, and O'Connor realised that Kerry needed to adopt a hard-working edge to their undoubted talent in order to compete with these teams. O'Connor also reshaped his forward line, with players like Colm Cooper and Declan and Darran O'Sullivan coming to the fore.

Kerry duly won the All-Ireland in 2004, crushing Mayo in the final.

In 2005, however, they lost out in a classic final confrontation with Tyrone. Doubts once again emerged about Kerry's ability to compete with their northern nemeses. And by the summer of 2006, revolution – Kerry style – was in the air when Kerry lost the Munster final replay to Cork and team captain Declan O'Sullivan was booed off the field by Kerry supporters. His presence in the team was questioned by many at the time, due to his close links to manager Jack O'Connor.

O'Connor subsequently changed things round and introduced Kieran Donaghy at full forward during the Qualifiers, the big target man offering an added dimension to the forward line upon his introduction. And the rest, as they say, is history.

Kerry went on that year to beat Armagh in the All-Ireland quarter-final and in doing so removed the myth that they could not beat a northern team at the time.

They hammered Mayo once more in the final, with Declan O'Sullivan returning to the starting 15 as captain and producing a stunning display. It is remarkable now, with the benefit of hindsight, to think that people actually questioned the claims of a player who went on to win 3 All Star awards in a row!

Pat O'Shea of the Dr Crokes club came in as manager in 2007 and he continued Kerry's winning run. Kerry were the first team to win back-to-back football titles in 17 years. The last Kerry team to achieve this was the 3-in-a-row side of 1986.

O'Shea was at the helm again in 2008 and came within a whisker of claiming the 3-in-a-row, but Tyrone once again prevailed.

When O'Shea opted to walk away from the position, Jack O'Connor returned to the hot seat and once again found a formula for success after a turbulent year.

O'Connor coaxed All Star defender Mike McCarthy out of retirement and also added Tadhg Kennelly to the panel, who returned from playing Aussie Rules and went on to win an All-Ireland medal and an All Star that year. Kennelly's achievement is truly one of the most remarkable in the history of the game, the Listowel Emmets club man being the only holder of both an AFL Premiership medallion and a Senior All-Ireland medal.

2009 also marked the retirement of Kerry great Darragh Ó Sé. It is no surprise that Kerry have struggled since the great man left the stage. Ó Sé, alongside his brothers Tomás and Marc, set the tone for a wonderful decade for Kerry football.

In the 10 years of the 'Noughties', Kerry played in 8 All-Ireland Senior finals, winning 5. I think few will disagree that the men of 2004–09 made up some of the greatest squads to have ever played the game. It would also be remiss of us not to point out that they won these All-Irelands in an era where Tyrone produced a truly great side that won 3 All-Ireland titles, while Armagh, Cork and Mayo also had top-quality teams.

6 Finals in a Row with 4 Wins

2004   26 September

| Kerry 1–20 | Mayo 2–9 | Croke Park | 79,749 |

2005   25 September

| Tyrone 1–16 | Kerry 2–10 | Croke Park | 82,112 |

2006   17 September

| Kerry 4–15 | Mayo 3–5 | Croke Park | 82,289 |

2007   16 September

| Kerry 3–13 | Cork 1–9 | Croke Park | 82,126 |

2008   21 September
Tyrone 1–15   Kerry 0–14   Croke Park   82,204

2009   20 September
Kerry 0–16   Cork 1–9   Croke Park   82,246

5 Football Facts

1. In 1975 Ger Power became the first official Man of the Match in a Senior All-Ireland football final.

2. 1979 was the first year the Man of the Match award was presented for the Senior County football final in Kerry. Paul Geaney of the losing (Castleisland District) team was the first recipient. Former Kerry keeper, Charlie Nelligan was full back and Castleisland captain that day, marking Austin Stacks' Mikey Sheehy. County colleague Ger Power was the winning captain that day.

3. Senior All-Ireland-winning medallist Tom Prendergast from Keel captained Kerry to a Munster senior title in 1972. Prendergast has a remarkable record, having also played Senior inter-county football for Wicklow in 1963, Donegal in 1964 and Cork in 1965.

4. Johnny Buckley was the first Kerry player to be black-carded in a Senior All-Ireland football final in 2014 against Donegal. Aidan O'Mahony was black-carded in the 2015 final.

5. Sean Murphy was best man at Mick O'Dwyer's wedding and Ned Fitzgerald (Maurice Fitzgerald's father and also a former Kerry captain) was best man at Mick O'Connell's wedding in 1972. O'Connell was married the day before the All-Ireland football final replay against Offaly.

THE MANAGERS:
1975–2019

Mick O'Dwyer is recognised as the first so-called 'manager' of a Kerry Senior football team. The Waterville legend took over the Kerry Senior football team in 1974 and his reign, along with that of his great rival, Dublin's Kevin Heffernan, saw the birth of the cult of the 'GAA manager'. Prior to 1974 Kerry had several 'trainers' who oversaw the team, including the distinguished likes of Johnny Culloty, Jackie Lyne, Dr Eamonn O'Sullivan and Jack McCarthy to name just a few.

The following is a profile of the 8 men who have held the 'keys to the Kingdom' over the past 44 years.

MICK O'DWYER
(1975–89)

'Micko' is rightly acknowledged as the greatest Gaelic football manager of all time. O'Dwyer's stellar inter-county championship playing career stretched from 1957 to 1973, but it was when he took over as manager in 1974 that the Waterville legend transformed Kerry's fortunes.

Kerry had endured a period where they had not won an All-Ireland title in 5 years, but Micko reinvigorated his side by fielding a team that became known as the 'Team of Bachelors'. Kerry went on to win 8 All-Ireland Senior Football titles in 12 years under his management. In that time Kerry won a 4-in-a-row and 3-in-a-row, and narrowly missed out on an historic 5-in-a-row when they lost to Offaly in the 1982 All-Ireland final. The 'Golden Years', as the period became known, is now synonymous with everything that is good about football. Kerry won 22 trophies during O'Dwyer's time in charge.

Micko went on to have successful stints as manager of both Kildare and Laois, thus cementing his reputation. As manager of the Kildare team in 1998, O'Dwyer led them to a Leinster title and an All-Ireland final; however, they narrowly lost out to Galway by 4 points in that final, having beaten Páidí Ó Sé's Kerry in the All-Ireland semifinal. He took over the Laois team in 2002, which he also led to a Leinster title in 2003 (the county's first since 1946).

Micko set the template in management in this county for others to follow, and he remains a true legend of the game, both in Kerry and throughout Ireland.

Micko's Championship Record: Games Played – 54: Won 41, Drew 4, Lost 7 – Winning percentage 76%

All-Ireland titles: 8; Munster titles: 11; National League Titles: 3

MICKEY NED O'SULLIVAN
(1989–92)

Mickey 'Ned' had the toughest job of all, trying to replace a Kerry icon. The Kenmare man was a teacher and also an expert in physical fitness, and he certainly appeared to be the right man to succeed Mick O'Dwyer at the time. It proved to be a difficult period, though, as the team were very much in transition, with Jack O'Shea and Pat Spillane the only recognisable players from the successful 1970s sides still around.

A Munster final win in 1991 brought renewed hope, but a defeat to Down in the All-Ireland semi-final was followed the next year by a catastrophic Munster final defeat to Clare. O'Sullivan left shortly after that loss, but went on to have a wonderful coaching career that included stints with the Limerick Seniors and the Kerry Minor footballers.

Mickey's Championship Record: Games Played – 9: Won 6, Lost 3 – Winning percentage 66%

Munster titles: 1

DENIS 'OGIE' MORAN
(1992–95)

They often say that timing is everything in sport and 'Ogie' Moran took over the Kerry Senior job at a time when Kerry football was in the doldrums. Kerry had infamously lost the Munster final to Clare the previous year and Moran came in to try to provide a boost to Kerry's flagging fortunes. The Ballybunion man is one of only 5 players to have won 8 All-Ireland Senior Football titles, but under his tenure Kerry lost 3 consecutive Munster finals to Cork by 3 points, 2 points and 3 points again.

It really was a case of being so near and yet so far. There certainly were signs of rejuvenation under Ogie, as he did bring in players like Dara Ó Cinnéide, Darragh Ó Sé, Mike Hassett, Johnny Crowley and Billy O'Shea during his tenure. These were players who all went on to have stellar Senior inter-county careers for Kerry.

Ogie's Championship Record: Games Played – 6:
Won 3, Lost 3 – Winning percentage 50%

PÁIDÍ Ó SÉ
(1995–2003)

The late, great Páidí Ó Sé will forever be heralded as the man who came in and ended 'The Famine'. Ó Sé cut his teeth in management at U–21 level with Kerry in the mid-1990s and the players that he moulded in that U–21 side formed the backbone of his Senior side from 1996 to 2003.

Páidí won his first All-Ireland Senior title as manager in 1997, ending the 11-year wait for an All-Ireland Senior title in the Kingdom. That win over Mayo will forever be remembered as the 'Maurice Fitzgerald' final, as the Cahersiveen man gave an exhibition of point-scoring that day. Kerry went on to capture a second Senior title under Páidí in 2000, when Seamus Moynihan led his team to a replay victory over Galway. Ó Sé soldiered on for another 3 years, but a loss to Armagh in the All-Ireland final of 2002 was followed by the West Kerry man's exit the following year.

Ó Sé did subsequently go on to manage Westmeath to an historic Leinster Senior Football title in 2004. This is still the Midlanders' only Senior provincial title.

Páidí's Championship Record: Games Played – 39: Won 28, Drew 4, Lost 7 – Winning percentage 72%

All-Ireland titles: 2; Munster titles: 6; National League Titles: 2 (won Division 2 in 2002); McGrath Cups: 1

JACK O'CONNOR
(2004–06, 2009–12)

The Dromid teacher never played Senior football for Kerry, but he quickly established in 2004 that he was a manager of the highest quality. In his first 3 years in charge, O'Connor guided Kerry to 2 All-Ireland titles, and he won a third in 2009.

He had also won an All-Ireland U–21 title as Kerry manager in 1998 and went on in 2014 to end Kerry's 20-year wait for All-Ireland Minor success. He won another All-Ireland Minor title the following year.

O'Connor is currently managing the Kerry U–20 side and he won a Munster title in 2018 with them before they narrowly lost to eventual champions Kildare in the All-Ireland semi-final.

Jack is the most successful Kerry manager of the modern era and his championship-winning percentage of 76% is only matched by the great Mick O'Dwyer. Kerry also won fourteen trophies during O'Connor's tenure.

Jack's Championship Record: Games Played – 46: Won 35, Drew 4, Lost 7 – Winning percentage 76%

All-Ireland titles: 3; Munster titles: 5; National League Titles: 3; McGrath Cup: 3

PAT O'SHEA
(2007–08)

Just like his predecessor, Jack O'Connor, Pat never played Senior inter-county championship football for Kerry. He did, however, have a highly decorated career with his club, Dr Crokes, which included winning the All-Ireland Senior club title in 1992. He is widely regarded as a top coach and it was no surprise when the Killarney man assumed the role of Munster GAA coach not long after retiring from playing football.

After Jack O'Connor stepped down as Kerry manager in 2006, O'Shea took over the Kerry Senior managerial position and in his first year in charge guided Kerry to All-Ireland glory. Kerry narrowly missed out on a 3-in-a-row the following year, losing to Tyrone in the final, and O'Shea subsequently stepped down after just a couple of years in charge.

Pat went on to guide his club to a second All-Ireland title in Croke Park in 2017, and in 2018 Dr Crokes annexed a 3-in-a-row of Kerry Senior Football titles under his leadership.

Pat's Championship Record: Games Played – 11: Won 8, Drew 1, Lost 2 – Winning percentage 73%

All-Ireland titles: 1; Munster titles: 1

EAMONN FITZMAURICE
(2012–18)

Eamonn Fitzmaurice began his career in Senior inter-county management back in 2012 as a raw, young 35-year-old. He began in impressive fashion, securing a first All-Ireland Senior title in 2014 in his second season in charge.

The Lixnaw man had an illustrious career as a player, winning Minor, U–21 and Senior All-Ireland medals with Kerry. He retired from inter-county football at the relatively young age of 30 in 2007. Eamonn went on to captain Feale Rangers to an historic county championship later that year. He was also Man of the Match in the final, as Feale Rangers beat South Kerry in a low-scoring game by 1–4 to 0–6, with Eamonn providing the winning point. Feale Rangers denied South Kerry a 4-in-a-row with that win. He also hurled for Lixnaw and won county championship hurling medals, as well as a Cork Senior Football title with UCC.

Eamonn stepped down as Kerry Senior manager in 2018. In his time in charge of Kerry his side won a 6-in-a-row of Munster Senior titles and also the

National League title in 2017 (memorably beating Dublin by a point in the final), as well as that All-Ireland Senior title in 2014.

Eamonn's Championship Record: Games Played – 31: Won 22, Drew 4, Lost 5 – Winning percentage 71%

All-Ireland titles: 1; Munster titles: 6; National League titles: 1; McGrath Cups: 2

PETER KEANE
(2018–)

The Cahersiveen man took over from Eamonn Fitzmaurice at the end of 2018. The former Kerry Minor manager had a spectacular start to his inter-county managerial career, winning 3 All-Ireland titles in a row and completing an unprecedented 5-in-a-row at Minor level. In his 20 games in charge of the Kerry Minor team he never experienced the taste of defeat.

Keane played Minor and U–21 football for Kerry and captained the Kerry U–21s to a Munster title in 1992, leading the likes of future Kerry Seniors Seamus Moynihan, Billy O'Shea, Pa Laide and Declan O'Keeffe in that U–21 side. He also had a highly successful club career as a player, winning 4 South Kerry Senior championship medals and also winning 4 county U–21 medals.

Keane has been joined in his back-room team by the likes of renowned coach Donie Buckley, as well as Tommy Griffin, Maurice Fitzgerald and James Foley as selectors. This group will be hoping to guide Kerry to a 38th All-Ireland Senior success in the coming years.

PANTHEON OF KERRY GREATS

In this section we salute some of the Kerry greats who have worn the green and gold with such distinction down through the years. Many more could have been included, but I am sure you will agree that this is an impressive list.

PRE-1950s

Austin Stack

The Tralee native was part of Kerry's first All-Ireland-winning side of 1903 and captained the team to All-Ireland glory in 1904. Stack's football career was cut short due to his political activity – he was a key figure in the Irish Republican Brotherhood in Kerry, and was commandant of the Kerry Brigade of the Irish Volunteers in the build-up to the Easter Rising. He died at the relatively young age of 49, but his name lives on in Tralee where the GAA county ground, Austin Stack Park, and also the local GAA club, Austin Stacks, are both named after the Ballymullen man. Austin Stack's name is synonymous with the game of Gaelic football in Tralee.

Dick Fitzgerald

The Killarney native played 58 times for Kerry, winning 5 All-Ireland titles along the way. Such was the impact that Fitzgerald made in Kerry GAA circles that our county ground, Fitzgerald Stadium, was named after him. The Dr Crokes player played

Senior football for Kerry from 1903 to 1923 and he captained Kerry to back-to-back All-Ireland titles in 1913 and 1914. He later wrote a book on Gaelic football entitled *How to Play Gaelic Football*, which was the first of its kind. Without question, Fitzgerald was one of the founding fathers of Kerry football and a true great.

John Joe Sheehy

The John Mitchels man was a member of the Kerry team from 1919 until 1930. Sheehy captained Kerry to the All-Ireland title on 2 occasions. His sons – Sean Óg, Niall and Paudie – all won titles with Kerry in the 1960s. He played in the Railway Cup Hurling final in 1927 and was captain of the Railway Cup football team the same year. Sheehy won 4 All-Ireland Senior medals and played 35 championship games, scoring 4–22. The road outside Austin Stack Park in Tralee is named John Joe Sheehy Road.

Joe Barrett

The Austin Stacks man was one of the stars of the great 4-in-a-row side and captained the team twice in that period. He actually gave up the captaincy in 1931, a gesture to his team mate – and former Free

State captain – Con Brosnan, as all sides of the political spectrum made an effort to unite under the banner of the Kerry Senior football team. Barrett was a rock solid full back who made 20 Senior championship appearances for Kerry.

Con Brosnan

Brosnan was a legendary name in north Kerry and the local GAA field in his native Moyvane is named after him. Con was a member of Kerry's 4-in-a-row side and he played 21 championship games for Kerry where he lined out mainly as a midfielder. Brosnan captained Kerry in their 1931 All-Ireland final win and remains one of north Kerry football's most famous sons. He put his political differences with many of his colleagues to one side to play football for his county.

John Joe 'Purty' Landers

Landers was another star of the 4-in-a-row team and played 32 Senior championship games for Kerry. He scored 11–20 in those games and was considered to be one of the greatest forwards to have ever worn the green and gold. 'Purty', as he was better known, won 5 Senior All-Ireland medals and played alongside his brothers Bill and Tim, who were all part of a star-studded Austin Stacks team at the time.

Jimmy 'Gawksie' O'Gorman

Jimmy was a member of the famed O'Gorman clan from John Mitchels. Thady O'Gorman had been the first All-Ireland Senior winning captain but 'Gawksie' was the most celebrated footballer of the family. He played in 3 All-Ireland Senior finals, winning all of them, and played 25 Senior championship games, scoring 8–22 from 1934 to 1943.

Dan O'Keeffe

Dan was named on the Team of the Century and during his long career the Kerins O'Rahillys keeper won 7 All-Ireland Senior medals and a record 14 Senior Munster championship medals. He made 66 Senior championship appearances from 1931 to 1948, which was also a record until Darragh Ó Sé surpassed him.

Paddy Kennedy

The Annascaul GAA club's home ground is named the Paddy Kennedy Memorial Park in his honour.

Regarded by many as one of the all-time greats of Kerry football, he was captain of the 1946 All-Ireland-winning team and made 45 championship appearances, scoring 5–23. Paddy won 5 Senior All-Ireland medals from 1936 to 1947 and, alongside Mick O'Connell, is considered to be one of Kerry's finest ever midfielders.

Paddy 'Bawn' Brosnan

'Bawn' was so versatile that he played full back, full forward and midfield for Kerry, all with equal success and ability. The Dingle legend played for 15 seasons from 1937 to 1952, winning 3 All-Ireland Senior medals. He made 40 championship appearances, scoring 2–6, and is one of the names synonymous with west Kerry football.

Joe Keohane

Keohane was still a member of the Minor team when he made his Senior debut in 1936. Over the next thirteen seasons, the John Mitchels man won 5 All-Ireland medals before retiring in 1948, having played 44 championship games. The debate still rages in Tralee as to who was the best ever Kerry full back – John 'Johnno' O'Keeffe or Joe Keohane?

1950s

John Dowling

The Strand Road legend captained Kerry to All-Ireland glory over the Dublin 'machine' in 1955. The tall and commanding midfielder won 2 All-Ireland Senior medals and formed a strong midfield partnership with Mick O'Connell. Dowling played 26 championship games, scoring 1–22 in the process.

Tadhgie Lyne

The Dr Crokes star played Senior football for Kerry in the 1950s, winning 3 All-Ireland Senior medals. Lyne was nicknamed the 'prince of forwards' and he scored 5–45 in 24 championship games. In his 3 All-Ireland final wins in 1953, 1955 and 1959 Lyne scored 0–12 in total and was known as a big game player at the time.

Seán Murphy

The man from Camp in west Kerry was selected as right wing back for the Team of the Century. Dr Seán played Senior football for Kerry from 1950 to 1961, winning 3 All-Ireland Senior medals along the way. Murphy played 28 Senior championship games in that time and is still considered to be one of the greatest wing backs to have ever played the game.

1960s

Mick O'Connell

The 'greatest' is a title that many attribute to the man simply known in Kerry as 'O'Connell'. The Valentia Islander played for the Kerry Senior football team from 1956 to 1973 and won 4 All-Ireland Senior medals and 1 All Star in his 56 Senior championship appearances. He is considered by many to be the most skilful footballer that the game has ever seen. Stories about O'Connell's enigmatic presence on and off the football field are legendary, and to this day he is still revered by Kerry football supporters.

Mick O'Dwyer

Long before Mick O'Dwyer became the greatest football manager of all time, the Waterville man was a Kerry Senior footballing star. In his playing career, Micko made 48 Senior championship appearances from 1957 to 1973. Micko was deadly accurate and scored 6–129 in that time. He also won 4 Senior All-Ireland medals. He backboned the Kerry side alongside Mick O'Connell in that era and was extremely versatile, as he could play in defence or attack with equal aplomb.

Johnny Culloty

The custodian was also Kerry's 'Mr Versatile'. He played hurling and football with equal ability. Johnny gained fame as an inter-county keeper who won 5 Senior All-Ireland medals in a career that spanned 16 years. He played 44 championship games and the Legion net-minder also won 5 county championships, 4 in football and 1 in hurling.

1970s

John O'Keeffe

'Johnno' was the prince of Kerry full backs. The Austin Stacks man was originally a midfielder, but he adapted to the role of full back with great expertise and is still considered the master of that position in this county. O'Keeffe won 7 All-Ireland Senior medals and 5 All Stars, as well as winning an All-Ireland Senior club medal with Austin Stacks. Johnno played 49 championship games for Kerry.

Páidí Ó Sé

Páidí's extraordinary playing career stretched from 1974 to 1988, winning a record-equalling 8 All-Ireland Senior medals along the way. The Ventry legend played in a variety of positions but was best known as a rampaging wing back. Páidí won 5 All Stars before going on to manage the Kerry Senior team to 2 Senior All-Ireland titles in 1997 and 2000. His nephews, Marc, Tomás and Darragh, all went on to emulate their uncle, wearing the green and gold with distinction.

John Egan

The Sneem legend was a goal machine, scoring 14 goals in just 41 championship games. His career spanned from 1973 to 1984 and he won 6 All-Ireland Senior medals along the way. John was Kerry captain in 1982 for the ill-fated 5-in-a-row attempt, but his career highs far outweighed the lows. John also won 5 All Stars. His son, John, is a current Irish soccer international and plays his club football at Sheffield United.

1980s

Mikey Sheehy

The doyen of Kerry forwards during the Golden Years era, Mikey scored a phenomenal 29 goals in 49 championship appearances. He remains the greatest goal scorer in the 131-year history of Senior championship football. He also shares the record of 8 Senior All-Ireland titles with 4 of his team mates. The Austin Stacks legend was also selected for the Team of the Century.

Pat Spillane

Spillane may be able to talk the talk these days on *The Sunday Game*, but he sure could walk the walk as well. Considered to be the greatest half forward to have ever played the game, the Templenoe man won a record-equalling 8 Senior All-Ireland medals and scored 19–23 in 56 championship appearances. His total of 9 All Stars is also a record in football and he was selected for the Team of the Century. After his playing career, Spillane forged a successful career with RTÉ as a presenter and analyst.

Jack O'Shea

The Cahersiveen legend was the ultimate box-to-box midfielder. He played 53 championship games and scored 11–53 from midfield. His goal against Offaly in the 1981 All-Ireland final is considered to be one of the greatest ever scored. 'Jacko' won 7 All-Ireland Senior medals and 6 All Star awards. He was selected for the Team of the Century. His all-action style of play became the template for modern-day midfielders.

1990s

Maurice Fitzgerald

Maurice is considered to be one of the most elegant footballers to ever wear the green and gold. Fitzgerald played 45 championship games for Kerry and scored 12–205. He made his debut in 1988 and went on to win 3 Senior All-Ireland titles, which included an inspiring Man of the Match performance in the 1997 win over Mayo, where he scored 9 of Kerry's 13 points. He is currently a selector with the Kerry Senior football team.

Seamus Moynihan

Kerry's millennium-year All-Ireland-winning captain was the inspirational leader of Kerry for over a decade. When he retired in 2006 he had won 4 All-Ireland Senior medals, played 61 championship games and won 3 All Star awards. The Glenflesk man was an outstanding half back but also excelled as a stand-in full back.

Darragh Ó Sé

The eldest of the Ó Sé brothers won 6 All-Ireland medals, more than any other Kerry player in the past 30 years. Darragh began his inter-county career in 1993 and it stretched for 16 championship seasons, when he signed off in style with an All-Ireland win against Cork. Ó Sé made 81 championship appearances for Kerry, scoring 1–30.

2000s

Tomás Ó Sé

Tomás won 5 All-Ireland Senior medals, 5 All Stars, 2 county championships in Kerry with An Ghaeltacht and also 2 Cork Senior medals with Nemo Rangers in a star-studded career. The attacking half back shares the all-time championship appearance record for Kerry with his brother Marc. Tomás played 88 times, scoring an impressive 3–35 from his defensive position.

Colm Cooper

The 'Gooch' won 5 All-Ireland Senior medals, 8 All Stars, 8 Senior county titles with Dr Crokes (which is a record he shares with Eoin Brosnan) and 1 All-Ireland Senior club title in an honour-laden career. He burst onto the inter-county scene as a raw 18-year-old in 2002 and played 85 Senior championship games, scoring a record-breaking 23–283. This total is the most scored by any Kerry player in the history of championship football.

Declan O'Sullivan

The Dromid Pearses star won 5 All-Ireland Senior medals in a career that spanned from 2003 to 2014. He also won 3 All Star awards and was considered the top centre forward of his era. He also captained Kerry to back-to-back All-Ireland titles, emulating Dick Fitzgerald with this achievement. Declan was a real on-field leader, playing 70 championship games for his county, and scoring 8–83.

2010s

Paul Galvin

The Lixnaw man and dual star played his club football with Finuge and had an outstanding career with Kerry between 2003 and 2015. In that time he won 4 All-Ireland Senior medals, 3 All Star awards and a Footballer of the Year award in 2009. He also captained Kerry in 2008 and was considered by many to define the new all-action, modern half forward. He made 58 championship appearances for Kerry, scoring 1–51 in that time.

Marc Ó Sé

Considered to be the greatest corner back of the modern era, Marc won 5 Senior All-Ireland medals and 3 All Stars, as well as winning a Footballer of the Year award in 2007. The youngest of the 3 Ó Sé siblings, Marc's Senior inter-county career stretched from 2002 to 2016. He made a record-equalling 88 championship appearances.

Kieran Donaghy

The big Stacks full forward burst onto the scene

in 2006 and was the mainstay of the Kerry Senior football team for over a decade. He has won 4 All-Ireland Senior medals, 3 All Stars and the 2006 Footballer of the Year in a glittering career. He made 69 championship appearances for his county, scoring 14–36, including goals in the All-Ireland final wins of 2006, 2007 and 2014. He announced his retirement from Senior inter-county football at the end of the 2018 season.

LADIES

Mary Jo Curran

Midfielder Curran was the on-field leader of the famed Kerry team who won 9 successive All-Ireland titles. She is considered to be one of the best players to ever grace the game. In 1980 and 1981 she won All-Ireland Minor titles. Curran won her first Senior medal in 1982 and from there went on to win 9-in-a-row. In those days, Kerry and Waterford were the top teams in the country and Curran recalls some of her toughest games being in the Munster championship. In 1991, when Kerry were going for the tenth title in a row, Waterford finally got the better of them in the Munster championship and then went on to win the All-Ireland. A couple of years later, Kerry came back to win another title, Curran's tenth, and after that she called it a day. She played national league basketball too, and kept that up after she retired from football.

Eileen and Margaret Lawlor

The Lawlor sisters were stars of the 9-in-a-row side. Originally from Ardfert, Margaret played alongside her equally gifted sister Eileen in the Kerry forward line. They both played their club football with Abbeydorney. Margaret won 4 All Stars in total and Eileen won 5 and they are both considered to be 2 of the best forwards to have ever played the game of Ladies football.

Marina Barry

Marina came into the 9-in-a-row side mid-way through their great winning run and quickly established herself as one of the top players of that era. She finished her career with 6 All Stars, which she won between 1986 and 1993. The Austin Stacks player was incredibly still playing club football and winning medals in recent years.

Geraldine O'Shea

The west Kerry player was a supremely gifted forward with sublime skills and she carried the Kerry side for many a year. She is widely recognised as one of the true greats of Ladies football in this county. Geraldine won 1 All-Ireland Senior medal, in 1993 in her debut year at the age of 16; she retired from the game 15 years later, in 2008. She also won 5 All Stars during that period.

TEAMS OF THE CENTURY/ MILLENNIUM

GAA FOOTBALL TEAM
OF THE CENTURY

The Football Team of the Century was chosen as part of the GAA's centenary year celebrations in 1984. This selection was based on recognising the best football players of the first 100 years. Nominated by *Sunday Independent* readers, the players were selected by a panel of experts and former players. Six Kerry players featured on the team – Dan O'Keeffe, Seán Murphy, Jack O'Shea, Mick O'Connell, Pat Spillane and Mikey Sheehy.

Full Team

Goalkeeper: Dan O'Keeffe (Kerry/Kerins O'Rahillys), All-Ireland SFC – 7

Right Corner Back: Enda Colleran (Galway/ Mountbellow-Moylough), All-Ireland SFC – 3

Full Back: Paddy O'Brien (Meath/Skryne), All-Ireland SFC – 2

Left Corner Back: Seán Flanagan (Mayo/ Ballaghaderreen), All-Ireland SFC – 2

Right Wing Back: Seán Murphy (Kerry/Camp), All-Ireland SFC – 3

Centre Back: John Joe O'Reilly (Cavan/Cornafean), All-Ireland SFC – 2

Left Wing Back: Stephen White (Louth/Cooley Kickhams), All-Ireland SFC – 1

Midfield: Mick O'Connell (Kerry/Valentia Young Islanders), All-Ireland SFC – 4

Midfield: Jack O'Shea (Kerry/St Mary's), All-Ireland SFC – 7

Right Wing Forward: Seán O'Neill (Down/John Mitchels), All-Ireland SFC – 3

Centre Forward: Sean Purcell (Galway/Tuam Stars), All-Ireland SFC – 1

Left Wing Forward: Pat Spillane (Kerry/Templenoe), All-Ireland SFC – 8

Right Corner Forward: Mikey Sheehy (Kerry/Austin Stacks), All-Ireland SFC – 8

Full Forward: Tom Langan (Mayo/Ballycastle), All-Ireland SFC – 2

Left Corner Forward: Kevin Heffernan (Dublin/St Vincents), All-Ireland SFC – 1

GAA FOOTBALL TEAM OF THE MILLENNIUM

This team, chosen in 1999 by a panel of GAA past presidents and journalists, aimed to single out the best 15 players who had played the game in their respective positions, from the foundation of the GAA up to the end of the 20th century.

When the GAA opened its new hall of fame section in the Croke Park museum on 11 February 2013, the members of this Team of the Millennium were inducted en masse.

Kerry once again had 6 players on this team, the only difference from a Kerry perspective between this team and the Team of the Century team picked 15 years previously being that Joe Keohane was selected at full back and Jack O'Shea failed to make the team.

1.
Dan O'Keeffe
(Kerry)

2.
Enda Colleran
(Galway)

3.
Joe Keohane
(Kerry)

4.
Seán Flanagan
(Mayo)

5.
Seán Murphy
(Kerry)

6.
J.J. O'Reilly
(Cavan)

7.
Martin O'Connell
(Meath)

8.
Mick O'Connell
(Kerry)

9.
Tommy Murphy
(Laois)

10.
Seán O'Neill
(Down)

11.
Sean Purcell
(Galway)

12.
Pat Spillane
(Kerry)

13.
Mikey Sheehy
(Kerry)

14.
Tommy Langan
(Mayo)

15
Kevin Heffernan
(Dublin)

KERRY TEAM OF THE 20TH CENTURY

Here is our Kerry team of the 20th century:

1.
Dan O'Keeffe

2.   3.   4.
Páidí Ó Sé   John O'Keeffe   Donie O'Sullivan

5.   6.   7.
Seán Murphy   Tim Kennelly   Mick O'Dwyer

8.   9.
Mick O'Connell   Jack O'Shea

10.   11.   12.
Maurice Fitzgerald   Tom 'Gega'   Pat Spillane
                                    O'Connor

13.   14.   15.
Mikey Sheehy   John Joe Sheehy   John Joe 'Purty'
                                                        Landers

MILLENNIUM MEN

There have been 19 All-Ireland Senior Football Championships in this millennium. Kerry and Dublin have each won 6 of those titles on offer, with Tyrone winning 3, while Cork, Galway, Armagh and Donegal have won 1 each.

Here is our Kerry team of the 21st century:

1.
Diarmuid Murphy

2.   3.   4.
Marc Ó Sé   Seamus Moynihan   Tom O'Sullivan

5.   6.   7.
Tomás Ó Sé   Aidan O'Mahony   Paul Murphy

8.   9.
Darragh Ó Sé   David Moran

10.   11.   12.
Paul Galvin   Declan O'Sullivan   Johnny Crowley

13.   14.   15.
Colm Cooper   Kieran Donaghy   Paul Geaney

5 Football Facts

1. Shane O'Sullivan from Laune Rangers has won 17 Mid Kerry Senior championship medals and that is believed to be a record for District championship medal wins in Kerry. Eoin Brosnan and Colm Cooper have both won 12 East Kerry Senior championship medals, and Bryan Sheehan and Austin Constable have both won 11 South Kerry titles.

2. Three players from Kerry's All-Ireland-winning panels of 1969 and 1970 went on to become radio broadcasters – Micheál Ó Sé (Raidió Na Gaeltachta and RTÉ), Liam Higgins (Radio Kerry) and Weeshie Fogarty (Radio Kerry).

3. 2018 All Star David Clifford had a memorable first appearance in the new Super 8s. Clifford scored 4–14 in 3 games against top-drawer sides Galway, Monaghan and Kildare. He converted 78% of his scoring chances, and all at the tender age of just 19.

4. Tadhgie Lyne played in an All-Ireland Senior final on 27 September 1959, the day after his wedding.

5. Jimmy Deenihan's last function as captain of Kerry was to collect the National League trophy in 1982. What was unique about that presentation was the fact that the future TD and minister was wearing the jersey of the beaten finalists, Cork, when he lifted the cup!

OTHER SENIOR
TITLES

THE NATIONAL FOOTBALL LEAGUE:
20 TITLES AND COUNTING

While the National League has always been seen as a secondary competition in Kerry, the county still has a wonderful record in the competition.

Kerry have won 20 titles in total. The nearest team to Kerry in the pecking order is, once again, Dublin, with 13 titles. Mayo have won 11, Cork 8 and Meath 7.

The National Football League was first held in 1925–26, which was 38 years after the first All-Ireland Senior Football Championship. Laois won the inaugural National Football League.

It did not take Kerry long, however, to get their hands on the League trophy. They won their first title in 1928 and repeated that win again in 1929, 1931 and 1932 (this counted as a 4-in-a-row, as the 1930 League did not take place).

Kerry also won a 4-in-a-row of League titles between 1971 and 1974. Strangely enough, we failed to win an All-Ireland title in that time and some Kerry fans reportedly began to consider winning the League a curse. We won the League again in 1977 and 1982 and did not win an All-Ireland title in either of those years. Unsurprisingly, the myth that winning a League was detrimental to Kerry winning an All-Ireland Senior title was at its height in that era.

That soon changed, however, when Kerry won the double of League and championship in the centenary year, 1984, and went on to do so again in 1997, 2004, 2006 and 2009.

Kerry have only lost 7 of the 27 League finals that they have competed in. Dublin's record in League finals, on the other hand, is worth noting. They have played in 26 finals, one less than Kerry, but they have only won 13, meaning it really has been a case of lucky and unlucky 13 for the Sky Blues.

League Titles Won – 20

1927–28, 1928–29, 1930–31, 1931–32, 1958–59, 1960–61, 1962–63, 1968–69, 1970–71, 1971–72, 1972–73, 1973–74, 1976–77, 1981–82, 1983–84, 1996–97, 2004, 2006, 2009, 2017

Top League Appearances

Legendary midfielder Jack O'Shea is the only Kerry player to have played over 100 League games for Kerry. The Cahersiveen man holds the record with 102 League appearances and it is debatable now whether that tally will ever be matched. Modern-day players are often rested for the League, but you can see that this practice has only been in evidence in recent times. The top 15 League appearances list contains a virtual who's who of star Kerry players over the past 50 years.

1	Jack O'Shea	102
2	Darragh Ó Sé	96
3	Seamus Moynihan	94
4	Mick O'Dwyer	93
5	John O'Keeffe	90
5	Tomás Ó Sé	90
7	Charlie Nelligan	89
8	Ger Power	85
9	Marc Ó Sé	84
10	Aidan O'Mahony	83

10	Páidí Ó Sé	83
12	Pat Spillane	81
13	Tom O'Sullivan	78
13	Sean Walsh	78
15	Mikey Sheehy	74

Top League Scorers

Mick O'Dwyer has scored more points in League football than any other Kerry player. O'Dwyer played most of his football in the forward line, but he did spend some time as a wing back, which makes his achievement all the more remarkable. Maurice Fitzgerald is third in the list, but his average of 4.4 points per game is the highest average of all the players in the top 10. Paul Geaney is the only current player in the top 20. The Dingle man has scored 10–74 in 28 League games and he is in 17th place on the all-time list.

1	Mick O'Dwyer	16–291	(93)
2	Mikey Sheehy	22–251	(74)
3	Maurice Fitzgerald	11–237	(62)
4	Bryan Sheehan	6–220	(64)

5	Dara Ó Cinnéide	11–180	(68)
6	Colm Cooper	11–158	(58)
7	Jack O'Shea	16–110	(102)
8	Brendan Lynch	11–124	(56)
9	Mick O'Connell	7–131	(73)
10	Pat Spillane	13–103	(81)

Kerry's 20 National League-Winning Teams

1928: Kerry 2–4 Kildare 1–6

J. Riordan, D. O'Connor, J. Barrett, J. Walsh, P. Russell, Jos O'Sullivan, Jas O'Sullivan, C. Brosnan, R. Stack, J. Ryan, J. J. Sheehy, E. Fitzgerald, E. Sweeney, Jas Bailey, J. J. Landers

1929: Kerry 1–7 Kildare 2–3

J. Riordan, D. O'Connor, J. Barrett, J. Walsh, P. Russell, J. O'Sullivan, T. O'Donnell, C. Brosnan, R. Stack, J. Ryan, J. J. Sheehy, M. Doyle, E. Sweeney, Jas Bailey, J. J. Landers

1931: Kerry 1–3 Cavan 1–2

J. Riordan, T. O'Donnell, P. Whitty, J. Walsh, P. Russell, J. O'Sullivan, E. Fitzgerald, C. Brosnan, R. Stack, C. Geaney, M. Doyle, J. Flavin, E. Sweeney, J. J. Landers, T. Landers. Sub: E. Barrett

1932: Kerry 5–2 Cork 3–3

D. O'Keeffe, D. O'Connor, P. Whitty, J. Walsh, T. O'Donnell, W. Kinnerk, M. Healy, R. Stack, J. J. Landers, T. Landers, M. Doyle, J. Ryan, J. Quill, W. Landers, C. Brosnan

1959: Kerry 2–8 Derry 1–8

J. Culloty, J. O'Shea, Jack Dowling, T. Lyons, S. Murphy, K. Coffey, M. O'Dwyer, M. O'Connell, Shas Murphy, D. McAuliffe, T. Long, P. Sheehy, D. Geaney, John Dowling, J. Brosnan

1961: Kerry 4–16 Derry 1–5

J. Culloty, Jack Dowling, N. Sheehy, T. Lyons, K. Coffey, T. Long, M. O'Dwyer, M. O'Connell, Shas Murphy, D. McAuliffe, B. Sheehy, J. Sheehy, D. Geaney, John Dowling, T. O'Dowd

1963: Kerry 1–18 New York 1–10

S. Fitzgerald, K. Coffey, N. Sheehy, Donie O'Sullivan, J. J. Barrett, Shas Murphy, J. O'Connor, J. O'Riordan, M. Fleming, B. O'Callaghan, M. O'Dwyer, D. O'Shea, P. Ahern, T. Burke, Denis O'Sullivan

1969: Kerry 2–33 New York 2–24

J. Culloty, Shas Murphy, P. O'Donoghue, S. Fitzgerald,

Donie O'Sullivan, M. Morris, M. Ó Sé, M. Fleming, D. J. Crowley, B. Lynch, C. O'Sullivan, E. O'Donoghue, T. Prendergast, L. Higgins, M. O'Dwyer. Subs: M. O'Connell, D. Crowley

1971: Kerry 0–11 Mayo 0–8

J. Culloty, D. O'Sullivan, P. O'Donoghue, S. Fitzgerald, T. Prendergast, J. O'Keeffe, M. O'Shea, P. Lynch, D. J. Crowley, B. Lynch, P. Griffin, E. O'Donoghue, M. Gleeson, L. Higgins, M. O'Dwyer. Sub: D. Crowley

1972: Kerry 2–11 Mayo 1–9

E. Fitzgerald, D. O'Sullivan, P. O'Donoghue, S. Fitzgerald, T. Prendergast, D. Crowley, M. O'Shea, M. O'Connell, J. O'Keeffe, P. Lynch, D. Kavanagh, E. O'Donoghue, M. Gleeson, L. Higgins, M. O'Dwyer. Subs: B. Lynch, J. Walsh, M. O'Sullivan

1973: Kerry 2–12 Offaly 0–14

E. Fitzgerald, D. O'Sullivan, P. O'Donoghue, J. Deenihan, G. O'Keeffe, D. Crowley, M. O'Shea, D. Kavanagh, J. O'Keeffe, B. Lynch, L. Higgins, E. O'Donoghue, J. Egan, M. O'Dwyer, J. Walsh. Subs: M. O'Sullivan, G. Power

1974 (replay): Kerry 0–14 Roscommon 0–8

P. O'Mahoney, D. O'Sullivan, P. O'Donoghue, D. Crowley, P. Ó Sé, P. Lynch, G. O'Keeffe, J. O'Keeffe, J. Long, E. O'Donoghue, M. O'Sullivan, G. Power, J. Egan, S. Fitzgerald, M. Sheehy

1977: Kerry 1–8 Dublin 1–6

C. Nelligan, J. Deenihan, P. Lynch, G. O'Keeffe, P. Ó Sé, T. Kennelly, G. Power, J. O'Keeffe, J. O'Shea, S. Walsh, D. Moran, M. Sheehy, B. Walsh, P. Spillane, J. Egan

1982 (replay): Kerry 1–9 Cork 0–5

C. Nelligan, J. Deenihan, J. O'Keeffe, G. O'Keeffe, P. Ó Sé, T. Kennelly, G. Lynch, J. O'Shea, S. Walsh, J. McElligott, D. Moran, T. Doyle, G. Power, E. Liston, J. Egan

1984: Kerry 1–11 Galway 0–11

C. Nelligan, P. Ó Sé, V. O'Connor, M. Spillane, T. Doyle, J. Higgins, G. Power, J. O'Shea, S. Walsh, T. O'Dowd, D. Moran, P. Spillane, D. O'Donoghue, T. Spillane, M. Sheehy. Subs: E. Liston, W. Maher

1997: Kerry 3–7 Cork 1–8

D. O'Keeffe, K. Burns, B. O'Shea, M. Hassett, S. Moynihan, L. O'Flaherty, E. Breen, D. Ó Sé, W. Kirby, P. Laide, L. Hassett, D. O'Dwyer, D. Ó Cinnéide, B. Clarke, M. Fitzgerald. Sub: M. F. Russell

2004: Kerry 3–11 Galway 1–16

D. Murphy, T. O'Sullivan, M. McCarthy, A. O'Mahony, T. Ó Sé, E. Fitzmaurice, S. Moynihan, E. Brosnan, W. Kirby, P. Galvin, D. O'Sullivan, L. Hassett, C. Cooper, J. Crowley, M. F. Russell. Subs: D. Ó Cinnéide for Crowley, M. Ó Sé for Galvin

2006: Kerry 2–11 Galway 0–11

D. Murphy, A. O'Mahony, M. Ó Sé, T. O'Sullivan, S. Moynihan, T. Ó Sé, M. Lyons, D. Ó Sé, K. Donaghy, P. Galvin, E. Fitzmaurice, B. Sheehan, C. Cooper, Declan O'Sullivan, R. O'Connor. Subs: Darran O'Sullivan, E. Brosnan, T. Griffin, M. F. Russell

2009: Kerry 1–15 Dublin 0–15

D. Murphy, P. Reidy, T. O'Sullivan, K. Young, T. Ó Sé, A. O'Mahony, T. Griffin, A. Maher, M. Quirke, D. Walsh, Declan O'Sullivan, Darran O'Sullivan, C. Cooper, K. Donaghy, T. Walsh. Subs: D. Ó Sé, T. Kennelly, B. Sheehan, D. Moran, Declan O'Sullivan, D. Bohane, S. O'Sullivan, A. O'Shea

2017: Kerry 0–20 Dublin 1–16

B. Kealy, F. Fitzgerald, M. Griffin, R. Shanahan, P. Murphy, T. Morley, P. Crowley, D. Moran, J. Barry, D. Walsh, M. Geaney, J. Lyne, J. Savage, P. Geaney, K.

McCarthy. Subs: G. Crowley, D. O'Sullivan, B. J. Keane, B. Sheehan, A. Maher, A. Spillane

Ladies National Football League

Titles Won – 11

1979–80, 1980–81, 1982, 1983, 1984, 1985, 1987, 1988, 1989, 1990, 1991

The Ladies National Football League was established in 1979 and Tipperary were the first winners. The 1980s were the golden era of Ladies football in Kerry, however, and the Kerry Ladies went on to win 11 of the next 12 League titles on offer.

The only spanner in the works came in 1986 when Wexford won the title. It must be remembered that Kerry also won 9 All-Ireland Senior titles in a row during that era. Kerry's last League title came in 1991 and they have not managed to win one since.

Cork have now joined Kerry at the top of the League winners list with 11 titles. Waterford are next with 5 wins, Monaghan have 4 and Mayo have 3 League titles.

THE McGRATH CUP

This competition was first run in 1981. The cup itself was donated by the late Joe McGrath from Cork to the Munster Council to assist in the promotion of Gaelic football in Munster.

The McGrath Cup is run annually as a pre-season competition and it has had many different formats and participants. In recent years counties have opted out of the competition for varying reasons and in 2018 Kerry decided not to defend the title they had won in 2017.

In the 37 years of the competition, Kerry have only managed to win it on 5 occasions. They first won the competition back in 1996 when Páidí Ó Sé was in his first year in charge of the Kerry Senior football team.

The win was made all the more enjoyable for Páidí and the squad as it came at the end of a long season and they could celebrate in London. Kerry did not win the McGrath Cup again until this decade, when they managed to win the trophy on 4 occasions.

Jack O'Connor was manager when they won

back-to-back McGrath Cups in 2010 and 2011. The McGrath Cup was also the first cup won by Eamonn Fitzmaurice as a manager in 2013 and Kerry went on to win it for a fifth time in 2017.

To some, just like the National League, the McGrath Cup is viewed with suspicion in this county. The startling stat still remains that Kerry have never won the All-Ireland Senior Football title in the same year that they have won the McGrath Cup.

Let's look at some of the names who have won McGrath Cup medals; it might someday make a great quiz question: 'What players won a McGrath Cup medal for Kerry, but did not go on to play Senior championship football?'

There are some good players on that list, such as Tomás Mac an tSaoir (An Ghaeltacht), Danny O'Sullivan (Kerins O'Rahillys), Pat Corridan (Finuge), Aidan 'Shine' O'Sullivan (Dromid Pearses), David Culhane (Ballylongford), Brendán Kelliher (Dingle), Pa McCarthy (Austin Stacks), Alan O'Sullivan (Dr Crokes), Podge O'Connor (Killarney Legion), Brian Looney (Dr Crokes), Eamonn Hickson (Annascaul), Michael 'Stam' O'Donoghue (Spa), Andrew Garnett (Spa), David

Geaney (Dingle), Alan Fitzgerald (Castlegregory) and Conor Keane (Killarney Legion).

This just goes to show the strength and depth to be found in Kerry.

Number of Titles

13 – Clare

9 – Cork

5 – Kerry (1996, 2010, 2011, 2013, 2017), Limerick

3 – Tipperary

2 – Waterford

1 – London

McGrath Cup-Winning Captains

Kerry's McGrath Cup-wining captains were as follows: Billy O'Shea (1996), Killian Young (2010, 2017), Tomás Ó Sé (2011), Anthony Maher (2013)

The Winning Scores, Teams and Scorers

1996: Kerry 5–17 London 1–6

Peter O'Leary, Killian Burns, Morgan O'Shea, Mike Hassett, Seamus Moynihan, Liam Flaherty, Eamonn Fitzmaurice, Joe Daly, William Kirby, Denis Dwyer,

Johnny Crowley, Pa Laide, Jack Ferriter, Donal Daly, Billy O'Shea. Subs: John Cronin for Ferriter, Mike Frank Russell for Billy O'Shea, Barry O'Shea for Moynihan

2010: Kerry 1–11 University College Cork 0–9

Ger Reidy, Pádraig Reidy, Tommy Griffin, Pat Corridan, Aidan 'Shine' O'Sullivan, Aidan O'Mahony, Killian Young, Micheál Quirke, Alan O'Sullivan, Paul Galvin, Declan O'Sullivan, Donnchadh Walsh, James O'Donoghue, Kieran Donaghy, Paul O'Connor. Subs: Paudge O'Connor for P. Reidy (inj, h-t), Barry John Keane for Paul O'Connor (40 mins), Seamus Scanlon for Quirke (45 mins), Kieran O'Leary for D. O'Sullivan, Brian Looney for D. Walsh (50 mins)

2011: Kerry 0–13 Clare 1–7

Tomás Mac An tSaoir, Pádraig Reidy, Marc Ó Sé, Pádraig O'Connor, Aidan O'Mahony, Tomás Ó Sé, Jonathan Lyne, Seamus Scanlon, David Moran, Gary Sayers, Darran O'Sullivan, Donnchadh Walsh, David Geaney, Michael O'Donoghue, Paul Geaney. Subs: Barry O'Grady for Sayers (h-t), Alan Fitzgerald for O'Donoghue (h-t), Danny O'Sullivan for O'Connor (55), Eamon Hickson for O'Mahony (57), Pa McCarthy for T. Ó Sé (62)

2013: Kerry 1–12 Tipperary 1–5

Brendan Kealy, Marc Ó Sé, Aidan O'Mahony, Shane Enright, Jonathan Lyne, Jack Sherwood, Tomás Ó Sé, Anthony Maher, Bryan Sheehan, Michael Geaney, Darran O'Sullivan, Michael O'Donoghue, Barry John Keane, Patrick Curtin, Paul Geaney. Subs: David Culhane for Sherwood (47), Andrew Garnett for Sheehan (57), Barry John Walsh for Keane (57), Paul Murphy for Lyne (58), Breandán Kelliher for O'Donoghue (59)

2017: Kerry 3–13 Limerick 2–12 (after extra time)

Brendan Kealy, Shane Enright, Jason Foley, Killian Young, Paul Murphy, Tadhg Morley, Tom O'Sullivan, David Moran, Jack Barry, Jonathan Lyne, Jack Savage, Michael Geaney, Barry John Keane, Paul Geaney, James O'Donoghue. Subs: Gavin Crowley for Murphy (29 mins, inj), Brendan O'Sullivan for Savage (44), Barry O'Sullivan for Barry (44), Brian Ó Seanacháin for M. Geaney (44), Denis Daly for Crowley (59, inj), Conor Geaney for O'Donoghue (64, inj), Conor Keane for P. Geaney (78), Kevin McCarthy for B. J. Keane (79), Adrian Spillane for T. O'Sullivan (82)

THE RAILWAY CUP

Kerry players have played a leading role in Munster's 15 Railway Cup successes down through the years. Munster have only won 15 titles in total, which when you think about it, is a poor return for a province like Munster in comparison with the likes of top dogs Ulster, who have won 32 titles, and Leinster who have won 28. Connacht is last on the list with 10 titles.

Munster have not won a Railway Cup, or GAA Inter-Provincial Championship as the competition is now called, in 10 years. Not one member of the current Senior football panel holds a Railway Cup medal.

Munster have only won 2 titles in the past 36 years. These wins occurred in 1999 and 2008.

Admittedly, the competition has fallen from grace in the GAA calendar. In its heyday, the Railway Cup was considered to be one of the most important competitions in the GAA. Huge crowds gathered to watch Mick O'Connell and Mick O'Dwyer lining up for Munster, opposite the likes of Kevin Mussen, Dan McCartan and Paddy Doherty for Ulster.

Munster Roll of Honour

Number of titles (15) – 1927, 1931, 1941, 1946, 1948–49, 1972, 1975–78, 1981–82, 1999, 2008

Kerry Players on Winning Railway Cup Sides

1927: Johnny Riordan, Joe Barrett, John 'Gal' Slattery, Jack Walsh, Paul Russell, Phil O'Sullivan, Con Brosnan, Bob Stack, Jackie Ryan, John Joe Sheehy (C), Tom Mahony, Jas Bailey, John Bailey, Dennis 'Rory' O'Connell, Eamonn Fitzgerald, Joe O'Sullivan, Frank Sheehy, Pat Clifford

1931: Johnny Riordan, Joe Barrett (C), Des O'Connor, Paul Russell, Tim O'Donnell, Con Brosnan, Bob Stack, Miko Doyle, Eamonn Fitzgerald, John Joe 'Purty' Landers, Tim 'Roundy' Landers, Paddy Whitty, Jackie Ryan, Joe O'Sullivan, Ned 'Pedlar' Sweeney, John Joe Sheehy, Jack Walsh, Dan O'Keeffe

1941: Dan O'Keeffe (C), Billy Myers, Joe Keohane, Tadhg Healy, Bill Casey, Eddie Walsh, Sean Brosnan, Paddy Kennedy, Johnny Walsh, Tom 'Gega' O'Connor, Murt Kelly, Paddy 'Bawn' Brosnan, Jimmy O'Gorman, Charlie O'Sullivan, John Falvey, Dan Spring

1946: Eddie Walsh, Paddy Kennedy, Willie 'Bruddy' O'Donnell, Dan Kavanagh, Jackie Lyne, Tadhg Healy

1948: Dan O'Keeffe, Joe Keohane, Paddy 'Bawn' Brosnan, Jackie Lyne (C), E. O'Connor, Tom Spillane, Willie O'Donnell, Batt Garvey, Teddy O'Sullivan, Frank O'Keeffe, Bill Casey, Eddie Dowling, Teddy O'Connor, Denny Lyne

1949: Teddy O'Connor, Paddy 'Bawn' Brosnan, Mick Finucane, Jackie Lyne, Eddie Dowling, Batt Garvey (C), Tom 'Gega' O'Connor, Tom Spillane, Tom Ashe

1972: Donie O'Sullivan, Seamus MacGearailt, Tom Prendergast, Mick O'Connell, Eamonn O'Donoghue, Mick O'Dwyer, John O'Keeffe

1975: John O'Keeffe, Ger Power, Paudie Lynch, Brendan Lynch, John Egan, Jimmy Deenihan, Mickey O'Sullivan

1976: Paudie O'Mahony, Jimmy Deenihan, Páidí Ó Sé, Ger Power, Denis 'Ogie' Moran, Mikey Sheehy, Mickey 'Ned' O'Sullivan (C), John Egan, Pat Spillane, Ger O'Keeffe, Pat McCarthy, Brendan Lynch, John O'Keeffe

1977: John O'Keeffe (C), Denis 'Ogie' Moran, Tim Kennelly, Paudie Lynch, Ger Power, Mikey Sheehy, Pat Spillane, Sean Walsh, John Egan, Ger O'Keeffe, Jack O'Shea

1978: John O'Keeffe (C), Ger O'Keeffe, Páidí Ó Sé, Tim Kennelly, Mikey Sheehy, Pat Spillane, Sean Walsh, John Egan, Paudie O'Mahony, Ger Power, Jack O'Shea

1981: Charlie Nelligan, Jimmy Deenihan, John O'Keeffe, Páidí Ó Sé, Tim Kennelly, Denis 'Ogie' Moran, Jack O'Shea, Ger Power (C), Pat Spillane, Mikey Sheehy, Eoin 'Bomber' Liston, John Egan, Sean Walsh

1982: Charlie Nelligan, Jimmy Deenihan, John O'Keeffe, Páidí Ó Sé, Tim Kennelly (C), Jack O'Shea, Denis 'Ogie' Moran, Sean Walsh, Mikey Sheehy, Eoin 'Bomber' Liston, John Egan, Tommy Doyle, Ger Power

1999: Declan O'Keeffe, Seamus Moynihan (C), Eamonn Breen, Darragh Ó Sé, Dara Ó Cinnéide, Liam Hassett

2008: Pádraig Reidy, Tomás Ó Sé

5 Football Facts

1. Brothers Kieran and Shane Murphy had a year to remember in 2018. Shane captained the Kerry Senior football team to Munster glory and Kieran captained the Kerry Junior footballers to Munster and All-Ireland honours. Then, on the same day in November, Shane won a Munster Senior club medal with Dr Crokes in Limerick, while Kieran won a Munster Intermediate Club medal with Kilcummin in Mallow.

2. Future TDs Jimmy Deenihan (Fine Gael) and Martin Ferris (Sinn Féin) won All-Ireland U–21 medals together with Kerry in 1973.

3. Former Tánaiste Dick Spring is the only player to have played Senior football and hurling with Kerry, as well as international rugby with Ireland. Dick played 3 National Football League games for Kerry, all as a substitute, in 1975.

4. In 1956 Tom Collins from Kilmoyley played

in 3 Munster finals on the one day. He played Junior hurling and Junior football against Waterford, as well as lining out for the Kerry Seniors against Cork.

5. 1993 was the first year that a Kerry captain took over the captaincy at the start of the League. Prior to that, the captain didn't assume the captaincy until the championship.

MINORS

THE HISTORY MAKERS:
MINOR FOOTBALL'S GOLDEN ERA

We have witnessed a golden era of Minor football in Kerry in recent years. Over a 5-year period, Kerry have remained unbeaten at this level, creating history along the way with a 5-in-a-row of All-Ireland titles. This was the first time that any male team in the 134-year history of the GAA had achieved a 5-in-a-row at inter-county level.

As hard as it is now to believe, prior to this run of success, there had been something of a 'famine' for the Kerry Minors, as they had not won an All-Ireland since 1994. The cracks at Minor level were covered over somewhat by the 7 All-Ireland Senior titles that Kerry won during that famine period.

Still, it became clear that something had to be done. And, to be fair, those responsible for the resurgence have done an unbelievable job. The underage Development Squads were structured properly and they began to produce a regular supply of quality footballers coming through to Minor ranks. This ultimately led to the current period, where Kerry have created history at Minor level.

In 2014, Jack O'Connor guided Kerry to a first All-Ireland title at this level in 20 years, and he went on to guide them to back-to-back titles the following year.

When Jack moved on to manage the Kerry U–21s, another south Kerry man, Peter Keane, came in. Keane had previously been a coach in that acclaimed Development Squad structure, and he went on to maintain the Minor's success, winning titles in 2016, 2017 and 2018.

This rich crop of young footballers have finally started to make the breakthrough at Senior level. Several individuals from the 5-in-a-row-winning sides have now gone on to make their debuts at Senior championship level. They are Jason Foley, Brian Ó Beaglaíoch, Tom O'Sullivan, Gavin White, Micheál Burns, Sean O'Shea and David Clifford.

Kerry's recent 5-in-a-row has also elevated the county to the top of the tree in terms of all-time wins.

All-Ireland Minor Titles

Kerry (16), Dublin (11), Cork (10), Tyrone (8), Mayo (7), Galway (6), Down, Roscommon, Derry (4), Laois,

Meath (3), Tipperary, Louth, Cavan, Armagh (2), Offaly, Westmeath, Clare (1)

Kerry's 16 All-Ireland Minor Football titles
1931–33, 1946, 1950, 1962–63, 1975, 1980, 1988, 1994, 2014–18

It has been an extraordinary period of success and all involved, like Donal Daly, the Games Development Administrators' various Development and Coaching Officers, and all the coaches at underage level, can take great pride in this success.

The trick now, of course, is to turn that underage success into Senior success.

30 STEPS TO HISTORY

Kerry's 30-match unbeaten run at Minor level is the longest unbeaten championship run in the history of the GAA. Kerry last lost a Minor championship match back in 2013 when Tyrone beat them after extra-time in the Minor All-Ireland quarter-final in Croke Park. Here is a year-by-year guide to that incredible period of success.

2014

This was the team that ended the 20-year Minor drought. The standout feature of this side was their all-round ability. Players like Tom O'Sullivan and Brian Ó Beaglaíoch have since gone on to make their Senior championship debuts but, in general, the rate of progress to the Senior ranks has been slower than some might have hoped.

Munster RD 1: Kerry 2–16 Clare 0–7; Munster SF: Kerry 2–18 Tipperary 0–7; Munster Final: Kerry 2–17 Cork 2–13; AIQF: Kerry 2–15 Kildare 1–8; AISF: Kerry 1–14 Mayo 2–7; AI Final: Kerry 0–17 Donegal 1–10.

Total Scored: 9–97. Total Conceded: 6–52. Average

Scored: 2–15. Average Conceded: 1–9. Average winning margin: 9 points.

Scorers: Killian Spillane 0–40, Jordan Kiely 5–6, Tomás Ó Sé 4–5, Micheál Burns 0–10, Liam Carey 0–9, Matthew Flaherty 0–8, Shane Ryan 0–4, Barry O'Sullivan, Stephen O'Sullivan, Brian Rayle 0–3, Cormac Coffey 0–2, Ivan Parker, Tom O'Sullivan, Mark O'Connor, Liam Kearney 0–1.

2015

This was the most miserly team of the 5 winning sides. They conceded an average of just 1–6 per game on their way to their All-Ireland win. The defensive cornerstone for success was supplemented by a strong midfield with captain Mark O'Connor and John Mark Foley, and a dynamite forward line led by Conor Geaney and the emerging Sean O'Shea, who has since moved up to the Senior panel.

Munster RD 1: Kerry 0–14 Clare 0–3; Munster SF: Kerry 0–16 Cork 1–12; Munster Final: Kerry 2–14 Tipperary 1–11; AIQF: Kerry 2–12 Sligo 1–6; AISF: Kerry 1–11 Derry 1–6; AI Final: Kerry 4–14 Tipperary 0–6.

Total Scored: 9–81. Total Conceded: 4–44. Average Scored: 2–12. Average Conceded: 1–6. Average winning margin: 9 points.

Scorers: Conor Geaney 4–27, Michael Foley 2–7, Sean O'Shea 0–8, Cormac Linnane 1–5, Bryan Sweeney 1–3, Stephen O'Sullivan, Gavin White, John Mark Foley 0-5, Brian Ó Seanacháin 1–1, Mark O'Connor 0–3, James Duggan, Billy Courtney, Daniel O'Brien, Ronan Buckley 0–2, Jack Morgan, Graham O'Sullivan, Evan Cronin, Brandon Barrett 0–1.

2016

The 2016 side was the team that most critics raved about, due to their free-flowing style of play. David Clifford, David Shaw, Dara Moynihan and captain Sean O'Shea simply terrorised defences. They could also defend as well, conceding just 1–8 per game.

Munster RD 1: Kerry 2–21 Waterford 1–2; Munster SF: Kerry 1–13 Clare 1–6; Munster Final: Kerry 3–14 Cork 3–8; AIQF: Kerry 1–24 Derry 2–10; AISF: Kerry 2–26 Kildare 0–10; AI Final: Kerry 3–7 Galway 0–9.

Total Scored: 12–105. Total Conceded: 7–45. Average Scored: 2–18. Average Conceded: 1–8. Average winning margin: 13 points.

Scorers: David Clifford 2–28, Sean O'Shea 2–25, David Shaw 2–11, Dara Moynihan 0–10, Diarmuid O'Connor, Ferdia O'Brien 2–2, Brian Friel 1–4, Mike Breen 0–4, Bryan Sweeney 1–0, Micheál Foley, Michael Potts 0–3, Niall Collins, Mark Ryan, Caolim Teahan,

Daniel O'Brien 0–2, Tomás O'Connor, Darren Casey, Cormac Linnane, Graham O'Sullivan 0–1.

2017

The 2017 side created all types of records. They had a phenomenal average winning margin of 16 points per game and also an average score of 3–18 per game. One man grabbed all the headlines and that was, of course, David Clifford. The Fossa teenager scored 4–4 in a never-to-be-forgotten display in the All-Ireland final win over Derry.

Munster RD 1: Kerry 2–16 Clare 1–6; Munster SF: Kerry 2–17 Cork 1–10; Munster Final: Kerry 2–21 Clare 0–3; AIQF: Kerry 1–22 Louth 2–9; AISF: Kerry 2–22 Cavan 2–10; AI Final: Kerry 6–17 Derry 1–8.

Total scored: 15–115. Total Conceded: 7–46. Average Scored: 3–18. Average Conceded: 1–8. Average Winning Margin: 16 points.

Scorers: David Clifford 8–41, Donal O'Sullivan 2–23, Brian Friel 1–17, Fiachra Clifford 2–8, Donnchadh O'Sullivan 1–8, Jack Griffin 1–5, Barry O'Mahony, Eddie Horan 0–3, Niall Donohue, Adam Donoghue 0–2, Cian Gammell, Michael Slattery, Diarmuid O'Connor 0–1.

2018

This was the first U–17 team to represent the county at Minor level. This team showed great maturity, despite some of the players being only 15 at the start of the campaign. This was a run to the final that was marked out by last-gasp wins over Cork, Monaghan, and even Galway in the final. Manager Peter Keane said this was 'the sweetest' win of all and few would disagree with his theory, as this was indeed a special – and historic – win.

Munster RD 1: Kerry 1–15 Tipperary 0–4; Munster SF: Kerry 1–11 Cork 1–10; Munster Final: Kerry 3–21 Clare 1–7; AIQF: Kerry 2–16 Roscommon 2–7; AISF: Kerry 1–16 Monaghan 2–11; AI Final: Kerry 0–21 Galway 1–14.

Total Scored: 8–100. Total Conceded: 7–53. Average Scored: 1–18. Average Conceded: 1–9. Average Winning Margin: 9 points.

Scorers: Paul Walsh 3–25, Dylan Geaney 2–13, Ruairdhri Ó Beaglaíoch 1–13, Darragh Rahilly 0–11, Killian Falvey 1–7, Paul O'Shea 0–7, Dan McCarthy 0–6, Jack O'Connor 0–5, Patrick D'Arcy 0–4, Jack Kennelly, Michael Lenihan 0–3, David Mangan 1–0, Darragh Lyne 0–2, Sean Quilter 0–1.

THE MANAGERS

Jack O'Connor

After 20 years of failure at Minor level there was only one name in the frame to take over from Mickey Ned O'Sullivan in 2013, and that was Jack O'Connor. Few could quibble with the choice, as results subsequently proved.

O'Connor added back-to-back All-Ireland Minor titles to the 3 that he had won at Senior level with Kerry, as well as the U–21 title he also won, to make him the most successful Kerry inter-county manager of the modern era. Jack surrounded himself with the likes of John Galvin, Micheál O'Shea, Eamonn Whelan, Arthur Fitzgerald, Alan O'Sullivan and, recently, former Kerry great Declan O'Sullivan. The mix proved to be a winning formula.

O'Connor was also at the helm in 4 All-Ireland schools winning sides, and his style of winning football played with a touch of flair and imagination proved a popular one with supporters. In the interim period Jack has moved up to the U–21/U–20 managerial portfolio, where he won a Munster U–20 title in 2018.

Peter Keane

Jack O'Connor was never going to be an easy man to follow but the choice of Peter Keane proved to be an astute one. Another man off the South Kerry managerial production line, Keane had an impressive track record in the build-up to his first inter-county appointment. He had guided St Mary's to an All-Ireland club title, had been a Kerry Minor selector under Mickey Ned and was also deeply involved at Development level.

During his time as Legion Senior manager, he guided the club to a first county final of the modern era, where they narrowly failed to defeat South Kerry after a replay. Keane has shown in his first inter-county managerial role that he is extremely well organised and a superb man manager. His sides play an attacking style of football that has earned huge praise both in Kerry and at national level. His astute choice of James Foley and Tommy Griffin as selectors, and Chris Flannery and Padraig Murphy as physical trainers, also added to what was already a winning formula.

Keane stepped down from his role as Minor manager in 2018, going on to succeed Eamonn Fitzmaurice as Kerry Senior football manager.

KERRY'S 16 ALL-IRELAND MINOR FOOTBALL WINNING TEAMS

1931: Kerry 3–4 Louth 0–4

Brendan Reidy, F. O'Neill, Paddy Walsh, E. Mahony, Dan Joe McCarthy, J. O'Keeffe, T. O'Sullivan, Jimmy O'Gorman, P. McMahon, T. Murphy, P. O'Sullivan, M. Buckley, Tim Chute, C. O'Sullivan, Bernie Healy

1932: Kerry 3–8 Laois 1–3

Brendan Reidy, F. O'Neill, E. Healy, J. Doyle, P. McMahon, Peter Ronan, S. McCarthy, J. O'Sullivan, T. Weir, P. McMahon, T. Wrenn, P. Ferriter, M. Brosnan, T. O'Leary, C. O'Sullivan. Sub: P. Lawlor

1933: Kerry 4–1 Mayo 0–9

Brendan Reidy, Michael O'Gorman, M. McCarthy, L. Crowley, S. Sullivan, Billy Myers, Timmy O'Leary, W. Dillon, S. Brosnan, E. Buckley, Brendan Cronin, Derry Griffin, W. Fitzgibbon, Paddy Kennedy, J. Counihan

1946: Kerry 3–7 Dublin 2–3

John Ryan, S. McCarthy, Bennie O'Sullivan, Donie Murphy, S. O'Sullivan, D. Sheehan, J. Fenton, Tom

Moriarty, Tom Ashe, M. Lynch, Dan O'Regan, P. O'Sullivan, Johnny O'Brien, J. Madden, Paddy Godley

1950: Kerry 3–6 Wexford 1–4

Donal M. O'Neill, Mike Galway, Mick Brosnan, J. Collins, Tomás Murphy, Paddy O'Donnell, Joe Kerins, Seán Murphy, Paudie Sheehy, Bobby Millar, C. Kennelly, C. O'Riordan, Brendan Galvin, Tom Lawlor, Paddy Fitzgerald

1962: Kerry 6–5 Mayo 0–7

Seamus Fitzgerald, Declan Lovett, Kieran O'Connor, Seanie Burrows, Ted Fitzgerald, Paud O'Donoghue, Bruddy Burrows, Denis O'Sullivan, T. Doyle, S. O'Mahony, A. Barrett, Derry O'Shea, John Flavin, Roddy O'Donnell, T. Mulvihill. Subs: S. Corridon, T. Kenneally

1963: Kerry 1–10 Westmeath 0–2

Seamus Fitzgerald, Tony Behan, John McCarthy, Seanie Burrows, Tom O'Shea, Bruddy Burrows, Con O'Riordan, Denis O'Sullivan, Georgie Curran, T. O'Hanlon, Arthur Spring, John Saunders, T. Kelleher, Harry McKinney, C. Donnelly. Subs: Mike O'Sullivan, S. O'Shea

1975: Kerry 1–10 Tyrone 0–4

Charlie Nelligan, Vincent O'Connor, Michael Colgan,

Michael O'Sullivan, John Joe O'Connor, Mick Spillane, Gabriel Casey, Sean Walsh, Neily O'Donovan (0–1), Fintan Scannell (0–2), Johnny Mulvihill (0–2), Robert Bunyan, Con O'Connor (0–1), Jack O'Shea (1–3), Paudie Sheehan (0–1)

1980: Kerry 3–12 Derry 0–11

Richard O'Brien, Davy Keane, Mike Crowley, Michael Counihan, Jamesie O'Sullivan, Tom Sheehy, John T. O'Sullivan, Pa O'Donoghue, Ambrose O'Donovan (0–2), Tom Dee (0–1), Joe Shannon (0–1), Liam Kearns (0–1), Tommy Parker (1–1), Willie Maher (0–4), Mike McAuliffe (2–1). Sub: Tom Spillane (0–1)

1988: Kerry 2–5 Dublin 0–5

Peter O'Leary, Peter Lenihan, Niall Savage, John B. O'Brien, Liam Flaherty, Vincent Knightley, Sean Walsh, Eamon Stack, Fintan Ashe (0–1), Pa Laide (0–1), Danny Cahill, Sean O'Sullivan (0–2), Colm Geaney (1–1), David Farrell, Billy O'Sullivan (1–0). Sub: Francis Doherty

1994: Kerry 0–16 Galway 1–7

Brian Murphy, Kieran O'Driscoll, Barry O'Shea, Sean O'Mahony, Timmy Joe Fleming, Charlie McCarthy, Fergus O'Connor (0–1), Denis O'Dwyer (0–2), Gene

O'Keeffe (0–2), Jack Ferriter (0–6), Liam Brosnan (0–1), Gerry Lynch (0–1), James O'Shea (0–2), Pa O'Sullivan (0–1), Gerry Murphy. Sub: Mike Frank Russell

2014: Kerry 0–17 Donegal 1–10

Shane Ryan (0–1), Dan O'Donoghue, Brian Ó Beaglaíoch, Tom O'Sullivan (0–1), Brian Sugrue, Andrew Barry, Cormac Coffey, Barry O'Sullivan (0–2), Mark O'Connor, Micheál Burns (0–2), Brian Rayle, Matthew Flaherty (0–1), Killian Spillane (0–5), Liam Kearney, Tomás Ó Sé (0–1). Subs: Liam Carey (0–2), Jordan Kiely (0–2), Robert Wharton, Stephen O'Sullivan, Ivan Parker

2015: Kerry 4–14 Tipperary 0–6

Billy Courtney, Darren Brosnan, Jason Foley, Tom O'Sullivan, Jack Morgan, Andrew Barry, Gavin White, Mark O'Connor (0–1), John Mark Foley (0-1), Brian Ó Seanacháin (0–1), Sean O'Shea (0–2), Brandon Barrett (0–1), Michael Foley (1–0), Bryan Sweeney (1–1), Conor Geaney (2–4). Subs: Stephen O'Sullivan (0–1), James Duggan (0–2), Mike Breen, Daniel O'Brien, Dara O'Shea, Graham O'Sullivan

2016: Kerry 3–7 Galway 0–9

Billy Courtney, David Naughten, Niall Collins (0–1), Graham O'Sullivan, Michael Potts, Daniel O'Brien,

Micheál Foley, Mike Breen, Mark Ryan, Dara Moynihan (0–2), Sean O'Shea (0–2), Diarmuid O'Connor (1–0), David Clifford (1–0), David Shaw (1–1), Brian Friel. Subs: Cormac Linnane (0–1), Caolim Teahan, Bryan Sweeney, Kieran Dwyer, Stefan Okunbor

2017: Kerry 6–17 Derry 1–8

Deividas Uosis, Sean O'Leary, Chris O'Donogue, Cian Gammell, Patrick Warren, Michael Potts, Niall Donohue, Barry Mahony, Diarmuid O'Connor, Adam Donoghue (0–1), David Clifford (4–4), Donal O'Sullivan (0–3), Fiachra Clifford (2–0), Jack Griffin (0–2), Brian Friel (0–5). Subs: Eddie Horan (0–1), Donnchadh O'Sullivan (0–1), Ciaran O'Reilly, Michael O'Leary, Ryan O'Neill, Michael Slattery

2018: Kerry 0–21 Galway 1–14

Marc Kelliher, Conor Flannery, Colm Moriarty, Owen Fitzgerald, Dan McCarthy (0–1), Dan Murphy, David Mangan, Paul O'Shea (0–2), Darragh Lyne, Darragh Rahilly (0–3), Patrick D'Arcy, Killian Falvey (0–4), Paul Walsh (0–4), Michael Lenihan (0–1), Dylan Geaney (0–2). Subs: Ruairdhri Ó Beaglaíoch (0–3), Kieran O'Donoghue, Jack Kennelly, Jack O'Connor (0–1)

U-21s/U-20s

KERRY AT U–21 LEVEL DOWN THROUGH THE YEARS

Kerry were the inaugural winners of the All-Ireland U–21 Football championship, which was played in 1964. However, this is the only grade of inter-county football in which Kerry does not sit atop the table of all-time winners. This is something that the Kerry GAA will be looking to redress in the years ahead.

Kerry have won 10 titles, which is one less than our neighbours Cork. Kerry have also competed in 17 finals, losing 7.

The U–21 competition has of course been re-graded now to U–20 and Kildare won the inaugural U–20 All-Ireland in 2018, defeating Kerry in the semi-final and Mayo in the final.

The new rules prevent players who are involved at Senior inter-county level from playing at U–20 level; as a result, Kerry missed out on a couple of key players, David Clifford and Sean O'Shea, in the 2018 championship.

Kerry have now gone 10 years without an All-Ireland win at this level.

Despite the new rules, it is certain that the U–20 side will still be very competitive, moving forward. And with Jack O'Connor at the helm, another title at this level might not be far away.

All-Ireland U–21 Football Championship Roll of Honour

Cork	11	1970,1971,1980,1981,1984,1985,1986, 1989,1994,2007,2009
Kerry	10	1964,1973,1975,1976,1977,1990,1995, 1996,1998,2008
Mayo	5	1967,1974,1983,2006,2016
Galway	5	1972,2002,2005,2011,2013
Dublin	5	2003,2010,2012,2014,2017
Tyrone	5	1991,1992,2000,2001,2015

KERRY'S 10 ALL-IRELAND U–21 WINNING TEAMS

1964: Kerry 1–10 Laois 1–3

Seamus Fitzgerald, Mick Morris, Paud O'Donoghue, Declan Lovett, John McCarthy, Vincent Lucey, Donie O'Sullivan, Denis O'Sullivan, Pat Griffin, Harry Mc-Kinney, A. Barrett, Derry O'Shea, Dom O'Donnell, J. J. Barrett, Sean Burrows. Subs: Ted Fitzgerald, P. Cahill

1973: Kerry 2–13 Mayo 0–13

Paudie O'Mahoney, Barry Harmon, Jimmy Deenihan, Batt O'Shea, Ger O'Keeffe, Ger Power, Kevin O'Donoghue, John Long, Paudie Lynch, John Coffey, Mickey Ned O'Sullivan, Páidí Ó Sé, Mick O'Shea, John Egan, Mikey Sheehy. Subs: Martin Ferris, Niall Brosnan

1975: Kerry 1–15 Dublin 0–10

Charlie Nelligan, Kevin O'Donoghue, Páidí Ó Sé, Gerard Leahy, Mick Spillane, Tim Kennelly, Denis Moran, Ger O'Driscoll, Sean Walsh, Barry Walsh, Mikey Sheehy, D. Murphy, Tommy Doyle, Jack O'Shea, Pat Spillane. Subs: Michael Ferriter, Tom Foley, Paddy Mulvihill

1976: Kerry 0–14 Kildare 1–3

Charlie Nelligan, Michael Colgan, Páidí Ó Sé, Gerard Leahy, Mick Spillane, Denis Moran, Vincent O'Connor, Sean Walsh, Jack O'Shea, Neily O'Donovan, Pat Spillane, Gerry Murphy, Barry Walsh, Ger O'Sullivan, Pat Foley

1977: Kerry 1–11 Down 1–5

Charlie Nelligan, Michael Keane, Vincent O'Connor, Mick Spillane, Denis 'Ogie' Moran, Johnny Mulvihill, Gabriel Casey, Jack O'Shea, Eoin Liston, Tommy Doyle, Sean Walsh, Pat Foley, Denis Moran, Tom Bridgman, Dan Coffey. Sub: Ger O'Sullivan for D. Moran

1990: Kerry 5–12 Tyrone 2–11

Peter O'Leary, John B. O'Brien, Sean Burke, Liam O'Flaherty, Pat Slattery, Vincent Knightley, Eamonn Breen, Maurice Fitzgerald, Niall O'Mahony, Pa Laide, Pat McKenna, Gene O'Driscoll, Pa Dennehy, Dave Farrell, Billy O'Sullivan. Sub: Paul Griffin

1995: Kerry 3–10 Mayo 1–12 (replay)

Diarmuid Murphy, Niall Mangan, Brian McCarthy, Barry O'Shea, Killian Burns, Mike Hassett, Charlie McCarthy, Darragh Ó Sé, Donal Daly, Denis O'Dwyer, Johnny Crowley, Mark Moynihan, Jack Ferriter, Liam Hassett, Dara Ó Cinnéide. Subs: Kieran O'Driscoll, Chris Drummond, Denie Dennehy

1996: Kerry 1–17 Cavan 2–10

Diarmuid Murphy, Kieran O'Driscoll, Brian McCarthy, Morgan O'Shea, Killian Burns, Chris Drummond, Eamonn Fitzmaurice, Darragh Ó Sé, William Kirby, Denis O'Dwyer, Liam Hassett, Dara Ó Cinnéide, James O'Shea, Brian Clarke, Mike Frank Russell. Subs: John Brennan, Ruairí O'Rahilly, Jack Ferriter

1998: Kerry 2–8 Laois 0–11

David Moloney, Mike McCarthy, Tom O'Sullivan, Kenneth Leen, John Sheehan, Tomás Ó Sé, Martin Beckett, Tommy Griffin, Eamonn Fitzmaurice, Aodán Mac Gearailt, Patrick O'Sullivan, Liam Brosnan, Mike Frank Russell, Noel Kennelly, Brian Scanlon. Subs: Ian Twiss, Mike Burke

2008: Kerry 2–12 Kildare 0–11

Tomás Mac An tSaoir, Colin O'Mahoney, Michael Moloney, Shane Enright, Aidan O'Sullivan, Killian Young, Gavin Duffy, David Moran, Alan O'Sullivan, Kieran O'Leary, Johnny Buckley, Michael O'Donoghue, Patrick Curran, Tommy Walsh, Paul O'Connor. Subs: Kieran Brennan, Eamonn Hickson, Brian Looney, Jamie Doolan, Eoin O'Neill

CLUB & DISTRICT FOOTBALL

ALL-IRELAND SUCCESS
AT CLUB LEVEL

The first Kerry side to win a club All-Ireland title was East Kerry back in 1971. That was the first year of the Senior All-Ireland club championship and so that team were the inaugural winners.

East Kerry is of course a District team. In Kerry, District teams compete alongside Senior club sides in the Senior county championship. There are 8 Senior club sides in Kerry and 9 District sides. A District team is a combination side brought together to compete. One example is West Kerry, made up of the best players from 4 club sides in the West Kerry District: An Ghaeltacht, Annascaul, Lispole and Castlegregory. Dingle, the fifth team in the West Kerry District, currently compete as a Senior club side.

After East Kerry's success, the GAA ruled that in the future only club teams could win the All-Ireland club title. Since then Dr Crokes have won the title twice with Castleisland Desmonds, Austin Stacks and Laune Rangers the other Kerry winners.

There are 5 championship grades in Kerry

football at present – Senior, Intermediate, Premier Junior, Junior and Novice. The advent of the All-Ireland Intermediate and Junior club finals, which were of course the brainchild of GAA President (and Kerryman) Sean Kelly, meant that even more Kerry clubs could strive for All-Ireland glory. While Kerry sides have sometimes struggled to compete at Senior level, the same cannot be said of Kerry clubs at Junior and Intermediate level.

Finuge was the first Kerry club to win an All-Ireland Junior title, in 2005, and Kerry have dominated that competition since, winning 9 titles in total.

At Intermediate level, Ardfert were the first Kerry winners, in 2007, and the men from the north Kerry cathedral village have won 3 All-Ireland club titles in total, making them the most decorated Kerry football club on the national stage. This is some achievement for a parish that is more renowned for their hurlers. Dr Crokes and St Mary's have won 2 each.

All-Ireland Senior Club Titles – Kerry winners: 6

East Kerry (1971), Austin Stacks (1977), Castleisland Desmonds (1985), Dr Crokes (1992, 2017), Laune Rangers (1996)

All-Ireland Intermediate Club Titles – Kerry winners: 6

Ardfert (2007, 2015), St Michael's/Foilmore (2009), Milltown/Castlemaine (2012), St Mary's Cahersiveen (2016), Kilcummin (2019)

All-Ireland Junior Club Titles – Kerry winners: 9

Finuge (2005), Ardfert (2006), Skellig Rangers (2009), Castlegregory (2010), St Mary's Cahersiveen (2011), Brosna (2015), Templenoe (2016), Glenbeigh/Glencar (2017), Beaufort (2019)

Munster Senior Club Titles – Kerry winners: 16

Dr Crokes (1990, 1991, 2006, 2011, 2012, 2013, 2016, 2018), Austin Stacks (1976, 2014), Laune Rangers (1995, 1996), Castleisland Desmonds (1984, 1985), East Kerry (1970), An Ghaeltacht (2003)

Munster Intermediate Club Titles – Kerry winners: 12

Ardfert (2006, 2014), Annascaul (2007), St Michael's/Foilmore (2008), Spa (2009), Gneeveguilla (2010), Milltown/Castlemaine (2011), Finuge (2012), St Mary's Cahersiveen (2015), Kenmare Shamrocks (2016), An Ghaeltacht (2017), Kilcummin (2018)

Munster Junior Club Titles – Kerry winners: 13

Finuge (2004), Ardfert (2005), Duagh (2006), Skellig Rangers (2008), Castlegregory (2009), St Mary's Cahersiveen (2010), Dromid Pearses (2011), Kenmare Shamrocks (2012), Keel (2013), Brosna (2014), Templenoe (2015), Glenbeigh/Glencar (2016), Beaufort (2018)

KERRY SENIOR COUNTY FOOTBALL CHAMPIONSHIP

Kerry's 'Mini All-Ireland', the Kerry Senior County Football Championship, will celebrate the 130th anniversary of its first game in 2019. The first ever football final was held back in 1889 and was won by Laune Rangers.

Kerry's county championship structure is of course unique, with 8 Senior clubs competing against 9 District sides. The District sides are South Kerry, Kenmare District, Mid Kerry, East Kerry, St Kieran's, St Brendan's, West Kerry, Shannon Rangers and Feale Rangers.

The 17 sides compete to win the coveted Bishop Moynihan Cup. The winning team still have the honour of nominating the Kerry Senior captain for the coming year.

Dr Crokes' victory in 2018 has seen them surge to the top of the all-time winners list with 13 titles, which places them one ahead of their great rivals, Austin Stacks.

The records tumbled with Crokes' win in 2018, as they became the first team to win 7 county titles in a decade, and they were also the first team to win a 4-in-a-row and a 3-in-a-row in the one decade.

Previous to this, in the 129-year history of the Kerry Senior Football Championship, no team had won so much as 6 Senior titles in a decade. Austin Stacks won 4 in a decade twice, while Dingle in the 1940s won 5. The great John Mitchels side in the 1960s also won the title 5 times.

Cooper and Brosnan Win Historic Winners Medal

Colm Cooper and Eoin Brosnan jointly hold the record for most individual wins in the county championship. They collected their 8th medals in Dr Crokes' 2018 county final win.

John Joe 'Purty' Landers and Niall Sheehy both won 7. Landers won his in the 1920s and 1930s, and was of course part of the great Austin Stacks side of that era. His first 2 medals came with a Tralee District team, however. Niall Sheehy's 7 medals were, of course, all with the one club, John Mitchels. Sheehy won his first medal in 1952 and then went on to win another 6 in the great 5-in-a-row side of 1959–63. He won his 7th Senior medal in 1966.

The record-holders, Cooper and Brosnan, won their first medals in 2000 and went on to be part of the 4-in-a-row from 2010 to 2013. Both of course were part of the current 3-in-a-row-winning team.

A number of the current Crokes squad now hold 7 county championship medals and it is conceivable that some of these players could go on to break the current record of 8 if Dr Crokes continue to be the dominant force in the Senior county championship.

Senior County Championship Roll of Honour

Dr Crokes	(13)	1901, 1912–14, 1991, 2000, 2010–13, 2016–18
Austin Stacks	(12)	1928, 1930–32, 1936, 1973, 1975–76, 1979, 1986, 1994, 2014
Laune Rangers	(10)	1889–90, 1892–93, 1900, 1911, 1989, 1993, 1995–96
John Mitchels	(10)	1929, 1937, 1947, 1952, 1959–63, 1966
South Kerry	(10)	1955–56, 1958, 1981–82, 2004–06, 2009, 2015

Tralee Mitchels	(9)	1896–97, 1902–03, 1907–08, 1910, 1917, 1919
East Kerry	(7)	1965, 1968–70, 1997–99
Kerins O'Rahillys	(6)	1933, 1939, 1953–54, 1957, 2002
Dingle	(6)	1938, 1940–41, 1943–44, 1948
Shannon Rangers	(5)	1942, 1945, 1964, 1972, 1977
Ballymacelligott	(4)	1891, 1894–95, 1918
Mid Kerry	(4)	1967, 1971, 1992, 2008
Feale Rangers	(3)	1978, 1980, 2007
West Kerry	(3)	1984–85, 1990
Tralee Division	(3)	1925–27
An Ghaeltacht	(2)	2001, 2003
Kenmare District	(2)	1974, 1987
Killarney	(2)	1949, 1983
St Kieran's, Castleisland	(1)	1988
Dick Fitzgeralds	(1)	1951
Castleisland Desmonds	(1)	1950
Killarney Legion	(1)	1946

Top Scorers in the Senior County Football Championship Final 2000–18

The following is a list of the top scorers in the 19 Senior county finals that have been played since the turn of the millennium. Pride of place goes to Mid Kerry's Gavan O'Grady, whose tally of 1–6 in the 2014 drawn final is the highest individual tally since 2000. Bryan Sheehan and Colm Cooper have been the final's top scorer on 4 separate occasions each.

2000	Eoin Brosnan (Dr Crokes) 1–0, Dara Ó Cinnéide (An Ghaeltacht) 0–3
2001	Darragh Long (Austin Stacks) 0–6
2002	Ger O'Brien 0–4, Declan Quill (both Kerins O'Rahillys) 0–4
2003	Mike Frank Russell (Laune Rangers) 0–7 (drawn game)
2003	Aodán Mac Gearailt 0–3, Dara Ó Cinnéide 0–3 (both An Ghaeltacht) (replay)
2004	Bryan Sheehan (South Kerry) 0–5
2005	Colm Cooper (Dr Crokes) 1–2
2006	Kieran O'Leary (Dr Crokes) 1–2

2007   Brian Scanlon (Feale Rangers) 1–1

2008   Kieran Foley (Mid Kerry) 2–2 (drawn game)

2008   Declan Quill (Kerins O'Rahillys) 0–5 (replay)

2009   Bryan Sheehan (South Kerry) 1–4

2010   Colm Cooper (Dr Crokes) 1–5

2011   Colm Cooper (Dr Crokes) 1–3

2012   Brian Looney (Dr Crokes) 1–3

2013   Colm Cooper 1–4, Kieran O'Leary 1–4 (both Dr Crokes)

2014   Gavan O'Grady (Mid Kerry) 1–6 (drawn game)

2014   Gavan O'Grady (Mid Kerry) 1–4 (replay)

2015   Bryan Sheehan (South Kerry) 0–7 (drawn game)

2015   Bryan Sheehan (South Kerry) 1–5 (replay)

2016   Paul O'Connor (Kenmare) 0–8

2017   Daithi Casey (Dr Crokes) 0–5

2018   Paul Geaney (Dingle) 0–6

KERRY INTERMEDIATE FOOTBALL CHAMPIONSHIP

There are 16 clubs who compete in the Intermediate championship in Kerry. At the end of the year the winners of the championship gain automatic promotion to Senior ranks, while one of the Senior clubs is relegated to the Intermediate level.

It is interesting to note that since the millennium only Dingle, Killarney Legion and Kenmare Shamrocks have won the Intermediate title and still remain a Senior side as of 2019.

List of Winners

2018 Kilcummin

2017 An Ghaeltacht

2016 Kenmare Shamrocks

2015 St Mary's

2014 Ardfert

2013 Currow

2012 Finuge

2011 Milltown/Castlemaine

2010 Gneeveguilla

2009 Spa

2008 St Michael's/Foilmore

2007 Annascaul

2006 Ardfert

2005 Killarney Legion

2004 Dingle

2003 Milltown/Castlemaine

2002 Listowel Emmets

2001 St Mary's

2000 Beaufort

1999 Rathmore

1998 An Ghaeltacht

1997 Kilcummin

1996 Annascaul

1995 Valentia

1994 Milltown/Castlemaine

1993 Waterville

1992 Annascaul

1991 Milltown/Castlemaine

1990 Kenmare

1989 Dingle

1988 Dingle

1987 Annascaul

1986 Valentia

1985 Dr Crokes

1983 Beale

1982 Annascaul

1981 Castleisland Desmonds

1980 Beaufort

1979 Castleisland Desmonds

1978 Castleisland Desmonds

1977 Tarbert

1976 Ballylongford

1975 Castlegregory

1974 Spa

1972 Ballylongford

1971 Ballylongford

1970 Kenmare

1969 Keel

1968 Kenmare

Note: The championship was not finished in 1973 and 1984.

KERRY JUNIOR FOOTBALL CHAMPIONSHIP

What follows is a list of the winners of the Kerry Football championship at Junior level from 1967 to the present day.

List of Winners

2018 Beaufort

2017 Dromid Pearses

2016 Glenbeigh/Glencar

2015 Templenoe

2014 Brosna

2013 Keel

2012 Kenmare Shamrocks

2011 Dromid Pearses

2010 St Mary's Cahersiveen

2009 Castlegregory

2008 Skellig Rangers

2007 Keel

2006 Duagh

2005 Ardfert

2004 Finuge

2003 Annascaul

2002 Finuge

2001 St Michael's/Foilmore

2000 Gneeveguilla

1999 Listowel Emmets

1998 Rathmore

1997 Sneem

1996 St Senan's

1995 Tarbert

1994 St Pat's Blennerville

1993 An Ghaeltacht

1992 Glenflesk

1991 Kilcummin

1990 Milltown/Castlemaine

1989 Brosna

1988 Currow

1987 Ardfert

1986 Cordal

1985 St Senan's

1984 Lispole

1983 St Mary's Cahersiveen

1982 Moyvane

1981 Valentia

1980 Beale

1979 Annascaul

1978 Gneeveguilla

1977 Beaufort

1976 An Ghaeltacht

1975 Templenoe

1974 Castlegregory

1973 Kilcummin

1972 Listowel Emmets

1971 Dingle

1970 Glenflesk

1969 Rathmore

1968 Keel

1967 Waterville

DISTRICT CHAMPIONSHIPS

North, South, East and West and of course Mid Kerry!

District Championships normally take place in Kerry at the end of the year. The 5 main districts are North, South, East, West and Mid Kerry. There are also championships played in the Kenmare district, however, and by the Tralee Town Board, as well as the St Brendan's Board.

These championships often mean more to players than any other in the season, and the pride of the parish is often seen when local rivalries come to a head, with passion the order of the day.

Victory in your own district ensures local bragging rights and is a key part of what makes Kerry GAA so special.

Many of these players play together during the year on both the inter-county and District teams, but that camaraderie and togetherness is always put to one side for the District championships.

With the new, streamlined GAA season the District competitions are now granted even more prominence on the calendar.

South Kerry Senior Championship (Jack Murphy Cup)

There are currently 8 clubs playing in the South Kerry District: St Mary's Cahersiveen, Valentia, Waterville, Renard, St Michael's/Foilmore, Dromid Pearses, Skellig Rangers and Sneem/Derrynane.

These teams compete annually for the coveted Jack Murphy Cup, with the winner earning the bragging rights on the Iveragh Peninsula for the following year.

The 'Townies', as St Mary's are often called, have the best record in the competition, and completed a 5-in-a-row at the end of 2018.

The Cahersiveen club is of course the home of famous players such as Jack O'Shea, Maurice Fitzgerald, Bryan Sheehan and current Kerry manager Peter Keane.

Next in the list is Valentia, home to one of Kerry's most iconic players, Mick O'Connell. The Islanders have won 21 titles.

Next in line is Waterville, who can count another Kerry icon, Mick O'Dwyer, as a former player.

As anyone unfamiliar with the geography of Kerry football can discern, there is football in

Kerry and then there is South Kerry football. The peninsula has arguably produced more iconic footballers than any other piece of land in Ireland.

Roll of Honour

St Mary's	(35)	1932*, 1937–38, 1940–44, 1947, 1949, 1952, 1954–55, 1960, 1969*, 1971, 1973, 1978, 1980, 1984–85, 1991–92, 1995, 2001–03, 2009–11, 2014–18
Valentia	(21)	1925, 1939, 1945, 1950, 1957–59, 1961–62, 1964, 1979, 1981–83, 1986–88, 1990, 1993, 2000, 2005
Waterville	(11)	1956, 1963, 1965–67, 1970, 1975–76, 1994, 1996, 1999
O'Connells	(5)	1903–04, 1929–31
Reenard	(4)	1948, 1951, 1953, 1989
Sneem	(4)	1972*, 1977, 1997–98
St Michael's/ Foilmore	(4)	2007–08, 2012–13
Skellig Rangers	(3)	1946, 1968, 2006
Derrynane	(2)	1928, 1936*

* Awarded championship.

Reenard/Foilmore (1) 1974

Dromid Pearses   (1) 2004

Unfinished: 1905, 1933, 1934 and 1935.

The 1902 championship was doubled with 1903, while the 1925 championship was run as a league and finished as a knock-out in 1926.

East Kerry Senior Football Championship (Dr O'Donoghue Cup)

The Dr O'Donoghue Cup or East Kerry Senior Football Championship was first played in 1954. The cup is named after Dr Paddy O'Donoghue, who was born in Glenflesk. He was educated at the local National School, at Presentation Brothers Cork and later qualified as a medical doctor at University College Cork and practised in Killarney. He gave outstanding service to the GAA as a player and administrator. He was President of the East Kerry Board from 1935 until his untimely death on 4 January 1948 at the age of 47.

There have been 65 finals played since 1954. Every year the 13 clubs of the East Kerry Divisional Board compete for the Senior championship title and they are as follows – Dr Crokes, Killarney

Legion, Spa, Fossa, Glenflesk, Rathmore, Gneeve-guilla, Cordal, Scartaglin, Currow, Kilcummin, Listry and Firies.**

Dr Crokes have won 30 titles in total. Next in line to the men from Lewis Road are Spa. Colm Cooper and Eoin Brosnan have won the most individual medals, with 12 each, taking over from Jackie Looney and Con Clifford, also of Dr Crokes, who won 10 titles each.

Roll of Honour

Dr Crokes	(30)	1956–62, 1964–65, 1968, 1981–82, 1986, 1990–93, 1995, 2000, 2002, 2004, 2006–13, 2018
Spa	(10)	1966, 1969, 1971–72, 1974–75, 1977, 1985, 1988–89
Rathmore	(8)	1963, 1978, 1984, 2005, 2014–17
Glenflesk	(6)	1988, 1994, 1996–97, 1999, 2001
Killarney Legion	(4)	1954–55, 1967, 1976
Gneeveguilla	(4)	1979, 1980, 1983, 2003
Kilcummin	(1)	1973
Currow	(1)	1998
Listry	(1)	1970

** Firies originally played in the Mid Kerry District.

Mid Kerry Senior Football Championship (Michael O'Connor Memorial Cup)

The Mid Kerry Senior Football Championship has 6 clubs contesting annually for the title. They are as follows: Beaufort, Cromane, Glenbeigh/Glencar, Keel, Laune Rangers and Milltown/Castlemaine.

The first final was played in 1947 and was won by Milltown/Castlemaine. Laune Rangers have dominated the competition over the years, however, winning 28 titles in total in the 70-year history of the competition.

Shane O'Sullivan (Laune Rangers) holds the record for winning the most titles. He has 17 Mid Kerry Senior medals. This is also a record in Kerry for an individual winning the most District championship medals.

Of the 6 teams currently competing in the Mid Kerry championship, only Cromane have yet to win a Senior championship title. The home club of former Kerry players Sean O'Sullivan and Donnchadh Walsh are still awaiting their first title.

Laune Rangers hold most of the records in the competition, including an 8-in-a-row between 1990 and 1997. Their last title, however, came back in 2006.

Roll of Honour

Laune Rangers	(28)	1958, 1963, 1966–67, 1969–70, 1973, 1983–88, 1990–97, 1999–2000, 2002–06
Milltown/ Castlemaine	(15)	1947, 1953–55, 1961–62, 1965, 1972, 1989, 2001, 2007–08, 2010, 2012, 2014
Beaufort	(9)	1976–80, 1982, 1998, 2016–17
Glenbeigh/ Glencar	(9)	1949, 1956, 1964, 1974–75, 2011, 2013, 2015, 2018
Keel	(8)	1948, 1957, 1959–60, 1968, 1971, 1981, 2009
Fries	(1)	1950

North Kerry Senior Football Championship (Eamon O'Donoghue Memorial Cup)

The North Kerry Senior Football Championship is a competition for GAA clubs affiliated to the North Kerry Division of Kerry. The official name of the competition is The Bernard O'Callaghan Memorial North Kerry Senior Football Championship, in honour of the late Bernie O'Callaghan (Beale) who was chairman of the North Kerry GAA Board for 25 years (1974 to 1998) and did a huge amount of work for North Kerry football. The championship usually runs from October to December each year but has on occasion continued into the New Year due to replays and postponements.

Fourteen clubs are currently eligible to play in the championship: Asdee, Ballydonoghue, Ballyduff, Ballylongford, Beale, Brosna, Castleisland Desmonds, Duagh, Finuge, Knocknagoshel, Listowel Emmets, Moyvane, St Senan's and Tarbert.

The championship is played on a straight knock-out basis. First-round games give home advantage to those first picked for ties during an open draw, with all further round matches being played at neutral venues.

Moyvane have been the most successful team in the championship with 18 titles. The prize for the winners is the Eamon O'Donoghue Memorial Cup. The cup is named after the Asdee native who starred for the great Ballylongford team of the 1960s and 1970s, and also for Kerry during that time.

Roll of Honour

Moyvane	(18)	1925, 1927–28, 1930, 1932, 1936–39, 1958, 1961, 1963–64, 1966, 1983, 1995, 1999, 2003

Listowel Emmets	(15)	1926, 1931, 1933, 1957, 1965, 1972, 1976, 1991, 1997, 1998, 2004, 2008–09, 2013, 2015
Ballylongford	(14)	1940–43, 1947, 1953, 1968, 1970–71, 1974–75, 1986, 1993, 2000
Ballydonoghue	(9)	1945–46, 1949–50, 1952, 1959, 1992, 2016–17
Beale	(8)	1977–79, 1981–82, 1984, 1989, 2014
Tarbert	(6)	1948, 1969, 1973, 1985, 1990, 2010
Duagh	(6)	1951, 1955–56, 1960, 1962, 2012
Finuge	(5)	1967, 1987, 1996, 2001, 2011
Castleisland Desmonds	(4)	1980, 1988, 2002, 2007
Ballyduff	(3)	1994, 2005–06
St Senan's	(1)	2018
Craughdarrig	(1)	1934
An tArm	(1)	1944
Faha/ Clounmacon	(1)	1954

The West Kerry Senior Football Championship (*Tomás Ághas Cup*)

The modern-day West Kerry Board was established

in 1957 with the first official West Kerry Senior championship final taking place in that year.

Over the years Blennerville, Kerins O'Rahillys, Churchill and Derrymore have entered teams in West Kerry competitions.

Nowadays, the West Kerry Senior Football Championship features 5 clubs. They are as follows: Dingle, An Ghaeltacht, Annascaul, Lispole and Castlegregory.

Roll of Honour

Dingle	(16)	1972, 1974–75, 1994–96, 1999, 2003, 2007, 2010, 2012–14, 2016, 2018
An Ghaeltacht	(16)	1960, 1965, 1967–70, 1991, 1997–98, 2000–02, 2006, 2008, 2015, 2017
Lispole	(9)	1978–79, 1982–87, 2004
Annascaul	(6)	1957, 1988–90, 1992, 2009
Dingle Pearses	(5)	1958–59, 1962–64
Castlegregory	(4)	1961, 1966, 1973, 1977
Kerins O'Rahillys	(1)	1980

5 Football Facts

1. Maybe there is a tradition in Kerry to give the captain time to prepare his All-Ireland-winning speech! In the years 1959, 1970, 1975, 1980, 2004 and 2009 the winning All-Ireland captains were replaced during the game. In 1959 Mick O'Connell was replaced by Moss O'Connell; in 1970 Donie O'Sullivan was replaced by Seamus MacGearailt; Mickey Ned O'Sullivan was replaced by Ger O'Driscoll in 1975 (Mickey Ned did not lift Sam, in the end, after leaving the field with an injury; Pat Spillane did so instead); in 1980 Ger Power was subbed and replaced by Ger O'Driscoll; 2004 saw Dara Ó Cinnéide being changed for Ronán O'Connor, and in 2009 Darran O'Sullivan was replaced by Kieran Donaghy.

2. Mick O'Connell captained Kerry to All-Ireland success in the 75th anniversary of the foundation of the GAA (1959). Ambrose O'Donovan repeated the feat in the centenary year (1984). Darran O'Sullivan lifted Sam on the GAA's 125th anniversary (2009).

3. In 1962 Kerry captain Sean Óg Sheehy won 3 Senior county championship medals in a 10-month period. June 1960 saw him win the 1959 Kerry final with John Mitchels; in October 1960 he won the Cork Senior county championship with UCC, and in April 1961 he retained the 1960 county championship with Mitchels.

4. Robert Bunyan (1975 Minor), Páidí Ó Sé (1985 Senior), Dara Ó Cinnéide (2004 Senior) all spoke completely in Irish in their All-Ireland-winning acceptance speech.

5. Tom Prendergast, Brendan Lynch and Johnny Culloty all won county championship hurling medals with Killarney 5 weeks after winning Senior All-Ireland football medals with Kerry in 1969.

COLLEGES
FOOTBALL

HOGAN CUP
(SENIOR COLLEGES ALL-IRELAND FOOTBALL)

Kerry Colleges football has never had a higher profile after a remarkable 4 year period of dominance between 2014 and 2017.

Pobalscoil Chorca Dhuibhne won back-to-back titles, and were followed of course by a back-to-back by St Brendan's, to complete an unprecedented 4-in-a-row of All-Ireland Colleges victories for Kerry.

In that short period of time Kerry doubled their Hogan Cup tally from 4 titles to 8. If you factor in that the county also celebrated an unprecedented 5-in-a-row of All-Ireland Minor titles during this time, it has undoubtedly been a never-to-be-forgotten period of dominance for Kerry at underage level.

Kerry's first Hogan Cup title was secured 50 years ago by St Brendan's in 1969. After a fallow period, the 'Sem' was once again victorious in 1992, and their success was followed by historic first wins by Intermediate School, Killorglin in 1996 and Coláiste Na Sceilge in 2009.

Those teams produced some of the true greats of Kerry football, like John O'Keeffe (1969), Seamus Moynihan (1992) and Mike Frank Russell (1996). More recently, current Kerry Senior stars like Tom O'Sullivan, Brian Ó Beaglaíoch and 2018 All Star David Clifford have also had success at this level.

Kerry's Hogan Cup Winners – 8 Titles

St Brendan's College, Killarney	(4)	1969, 1992, 2016, 2017
Pobalscoil Chorca Dhuibhne, Daingean Uí Chúis	(2)	2014, 2015
Coláiste Na Sceilge, Cahersiveen	(1)	2009
Intermediate School, Killorglin	(1)	1996

The Finals

1969

St Brendan's, Killarney 1–13
St Mary's, Galway 3–3

The Sem will celebrate the 50th anniversary of the first Kerry side to win a Hogan Cup in 2019. The team were captained by the legend that is John O'Keeffe. The future Kerry star gave an incredible display that day. The Sem conceded 3 goals but had the scoring dash to blitz past St Mary's of Galway by 1–13 to 3–3. The 'Sem' team was trained by Fr James Linnane and included future Kerry County Board secretary Tony O'Keeffe and his brother, and future Kerry captain, Ger O'Keeffe. Their future inter-county colleague Paudie Lynch was another star of that historic first Hogan Cup-winning side.

St Brendan's: John Foley, Tony O'Keeffe, Donal McMahon, Tom Hanafin, John J. McCarthy, John O'Keeffe, Ger O'Keeffe, Paudie Lynch, John Long, Don Kissane, Charles O'Connor, Tom Looney, Denis O'Keeffe, Ciaran Sugrue, Pat Lucey. Subs: Paudie O'Mahony, Ted Kennelly, Niall Brosnan, Joe Buckley, Jim Cremin, Bernard Dennehy, Paud O'Donoghue

1992

St Brendan's, Killarney 0–9
St Jarlath's College, Tuam 0–5

Backboned by Seamus Moynihan, Killian Burns, Ruairí O'Rahilly, captain Niall Mangan and future Kerry hurler and Causeway native Maurice Harty, St Brendan's saw off Sacred Heart, Carraig na bhFear, by a whopping 2–13 to 0–8 in the semi-final, but the mighty St Jarlath's were expected, and proved, to be a different proposition. St Jarlath's had beaten the 'Sem' in the semi-finals on no less than 4 previous meetings: 1946, 1947, 1973 and 1974. This time around, however, it was the Killarney college that prevailed.

St Brendan's: Liam O'Sullivan, Killian Burns, Niall Mangan, Denis Doody, Eamon O'Sullivan, Brian McCarthy, Brendan Fitzgerald, Seamus Moynihan, Maurice Harty, John Dorgan, Tony McManus, Ruairí O'Rahilly, Conor O'Donnell, Tom Stack, John Doyle. Subs: Moss Murphy, Darren Counihan, Timmy O'Sullivan, Ted Bowler, Morgan O'Shea, Daire O'Connor, Conor McSweeney, Padraig Teahan, Timmy O'Sullivan

1996

Intermediate School, Killorglin 4–8
St Patrick's College, Maghera 1–14

ISK, who just over 5 years previously were only deemed good enough to play 'C' grade, completed a fairytale ride to the top by claiming the All-Ireland Colleges Senior football championship crown in an absorbing final at Croke Park.

The match proved to be a clash of two cultures: Killorglin's speed and finesse colliding with

Maghera's greater physical strength. Three of Laune Rangers' All-Ireland club winners from the previous month (Pat O'Sullivan, John Sheehan and Michael Francis Russell) were also part of this success.

Intermediate School (full panel): Pat Healy, Eoin O'Connell, Jimmy Doyle, Ryan Kinnerk, John Moriarty, John Sheehan, Eanna O'Malley, John Lynch, Pa O'Sullivan, Mike Frank Russell, Mike Kelliher, Pat Leahy, Garret Sheehan, Fergal O'Brien, John O'Connor, Brendan Fitzgerald, Shane Harmon, Tony Lyons, Diarmuid O'Sullivan, Michael Ahern, Eoin Clifford, Enda Clifford, John Ahern, Tim Moriarty, Daniel O'Shea, Ger Moriarty, Tim Scannell, Keith McKenna

2009

Coláiste Na Sceilge, Cahersiveen, 1–9
St Mary's College, Edenderry 0–10

A 62nd-minute goal from Éanna O'Connor, son of former Kerry Senior manager Jack O'Connor, ensured Coláiste na Sceilge their first Hogan Cup title at O'Moore Park, Portlaoise. O'Connor, now based in Kildare with Moorefield, was top scorer with 1–2 on the day.

Coláiste Na Sceilge: Damian Horgan, Stephen O'Sullivan, Mark Griffin, Niall Fitzgerald, Shane O'Sullivan,

Dominic O'Sullivan, Ian Casey, Max Thiemann, Greg Gibson, Ian Galvin (0–1), Damian Kelly (0–2), Daniel Daly, Stephen O'Dwyer (0–2), Éanna O'Connor (1–2), Niall O'Shea (0–2). Sub: Barry O'Dwyer for Stephen O'Sullivan (49)

2014

Pobalscoil Chorca Dhuibhne, Daingean Uí Chúis 1–8
St Patrick's College, Maghera 1–6

Pobalscoil Chorca Dhuibhne captured their first GAA All-Ireland Post-Primary Schools Senior 'A' football title in Croke Park in a ferocious battle. The Derry school had led by as many as 6 points in the first half, as they benefited from wayward shooting from a Kerry side who failed to trouble the score-board operators until the 20th minute, when Séamus Ó Muircheartaigh pointed. Eventually, though, the Dingle team, who were managed by future Kerry Senior manager Eamonn Fitzmaurice, found their range and Barra Ó Súilleabháin's late score secured a famous win for the West Kerry students.

Pobalscoil Chorca Dhuibhne: Dáithí Ó Conchúir, Conchúir Ó Súilleabháin, Brian Ó Beaglaíoch, Tom Ó Súilleabháin (0–2, 2f), Maitiú Ó Flatharta (0–1),

Caoimhghin Ó Beaglaíoch, Seán Ó Gairbhia, Barra Ó Súilleabháin (0–1), Marc Ó Conchúir, Roibeárd Ó Sé (1–0), Brian Ó Raoil, Séamus Ó Muircheartaigh (0–3, 2f), Conchúir Ó Géibheannaigh, Cathal Ó Bambaire, Tomás Ó Sé (0–1). Subs: Cian Ó Murchú for Ó Géibheannaigh (h-t)

2015

Pobalscoil Chorca Dhuibhne, Daingean Uí Chúis 1–12
CBS, Roscommon 2–5

The West Kerry college made it back-to-back Hogan Cup titles in this year. Eamonn Fitzmaurice had now departed the scene, with his former right-hand man and future Kerry Minor and Senior coach Tommy Griffin now in charge. The Dingle school managed to hold off a strong challenge from the Roscommon lads on the day in Croke Park.

Pobalscoil Chorca Dhuibhne: Lúcás De Bhailís, Conor O'Sullivan, Tom Leo O'Sullivan, Cian Ó Murchú, Aidan O'Connor, Brian Ó Beaglaíoch (0–1), Tom O'Sullivan, Mark O'Connor, Pádraig Mac a'tSithigh, Máirtin Ó Gormáin (0–1), Sean Ó Gairbhia (1–1), P.J. Mac Láimh, Cathal Bambury (0–1), Séamus Ó Muircheartaigh (0–2, 2f), Conor Geaney (0–5, 3f). Subs: Gearóid Hicí

Ó Brosnacháin (0–1) for Mac Láimh (h-t), Ryan Ó Mainnín for Mac a'tSithigh (53)

2016

St Brendan's, Killarney 2–13
St Patrick's College, Maghera 2–6

This was the final in which a young David Clifford first burst onto the national consciousness. The future All Star scored 2–5 in this win, including a wonder goal that will live long in the memory, where he won the ball in front of an empty Hill Sixteen end, beat his man and sent a superb shot with his left foot to the roof of the net. Victory meant that the Sem bridged the 24-year gap to their previous success in the Hogan Cup in 1992.

St Brendan's: David Carroll, Cian Gammell, Daniel O'Brien, Chris O'Donoghue, Niall Donohue, David Naughton, Michael Potts, Lee O'Donoghue (0–1), Billy Courtney, Peter McCarthy, David Clifford (2–5), Dara Moynihan (0–4), Evan Cronin (0–1), David Shaw (0–1), Michael Casey (0–1). Subs: William Courtney for Casey (43), David Spillane for McCarthy (60)

2017

St Brendan's, Killarney 0–18
St Peter's College, Wexford 0–10

The Sem retained their Hogan Cup title and claimed a fourth overall with an 8-point victory over St Peter's in Croke Park. This win also made it 4 wins in a row for Kerry Colleges at this level.

Garry McGrath's side were full value for the win, which never looked in doubt. A free-flowing St Brendan's attack was in complete control at half-time, leading by 0–10 to 0–3. St Peter's rallied after the break and found themselves just 4 points in arrears with 10 minutes remaining, but St Brendan's put the foot on the accelerator and eased home with an 8-point margin.

St Brendan's: Robert Osborne, Lorcan McMonagle, Chris O'Donoghue, Sean O'Leary, Jack Griffin (0–1), Michael Potts, Niall Donohue, Billy Courtney (0–4), Cian Gammell, Dara Moynihan (0–2), Donnchadh O'Sullivan (0–4), Barry Keane, David Shaw (0–4), Mark O'Shea (0–1), Ciaran Flynn (0–1). Subs: Micheál Devlin (0–1) for Flynn (44), Barry Slattery for O'Donoghue (blood sub, 52–59), Mark Harnett for Keane (55), Evan Cosgrove for Griffin (61), Niall McCarthy for O'Shea (62), Diarmuid Brosnan for McMonagle (63)

CORN UÍ MHUIRÍ:

48 SENIOR FOOTBALL COLLEGES TITLES FOR KERRY COLLEGES

The Corn Uí Mhuirí has long been seen as a breeding ground for future Kerry Senior football stars. Over the years Kerry Colleges have dominated the Munster post-primary schools Senior 'A' competition, with St Brendan's, Killarney, winning a record-breaking 22 titles.

Their first win came way back in 1929, but it was CBS High School Clonmel who were the very first winners of this historic competition that celebrated its 90th year in 2018.

Tralee CBS are next in the list of overall winners, alongside Coláiste Chríost Rí from Cork with 15 titles each.

Roll of Honour – Kerry's 46 Corn Uí Mhuirí titles

St Brendan's, Killarney	(22)	1929–30, 1937–38, 1942–43, 1946–47, 1963, 1966, 1969, 1972–74, 1977, 1986,1992, 1994, 2008, 2010, 2016–17

Tralee CBS	(15)	1931–34, 1940–41, 1944–45, 1948, 1953, 1955, 1976, 1999, 2000, 2007
Pobalscoil Chorca Dhuibhne	(6)	2012–15, 2018, 2019
Coláiste Na Sceilge, Cahersiveen	(4)	2001–03, 2009
Intermediate School, Killorglin	(1)	1996

INTERNATIONAL
RULES

KERRY'S PARTICIPATION IN INTERNATIONAL RULES

The International Rules Series is a Senior men's international rules football competition played between the Australia international rules football team (selected by the Australian Football League) and the Ireland international rules football team (selected by the GAA). The series is played intermittently – normally in October or November – after the completion of the AFL Grand Final and the All-Ireland football final.

The matches are played using a set of compromise rules decided upon by both governing bodies, and is known formally as 'international rules football'. The teams contest for a trophy, which in 2004 was named the Cormac McAnallen Cup after the Tyrone team captain Cormac McAnallen, whose death that year from a heart condition came after he had represented Ireland in the previous 3 series.

The concept for the series originates from the Australian Football World Tour, which took place in 1967. The first series took place in Ireland in 1984 under a 3-match format. Following poor

Australian crowds and a relative lack of interest, the series was cancelled in 1990. It was revived in 1998, however, under a two-match, aggregate-points format.

The tests were indefinitely postponed again by the GAA in 2007 following the 2006 series, citing a series of violent on-field incidents. However, the series resumed in October 2008 in Australia, after the GAA and AFL reached collective agreement on a revised set of rules.

The all-time series count is a tie with Ireland and Australia both on 10 wins. There have been 40 tests in total and Ireland just tip the balance here, having won 21 to Australia's 19.

Here are the details that are to hand on the series played over the past 35 years. In that time, Kerry's Tadhg Kennelly played in 6 series, Seamus Moynihan in 5, with Tom Spillane, Darragh Ó Sé and Kieran Donaghy playing in 3 series each.

1984

This was the first official series between Gaelic footballers from Ireland and Australian rules footballers from Australia. The Australian team won the test series 2–1 and finished with a superior aggregate of 222 points to Ireland's 208. Dublin's former manager Kevin Heffernan was the Irish manager.

Kerry – Eoin Liston, Jack O'Shea, Tom Spillane, Sean Walsh, Charlie Nelligan

1986

Kevin Heffernan was once again the manager, the series taking place in Australia for the first time. Ireland won the series 3–0 and by 32 points over the 3 test matches.

Kerry – Jack O'Shea, Pat Spillane, Tom Spillane

1987

The series took place in Ireland, again consisting of 3 test matches. Australia won the series 2–1 and by 23 points over the test matches.

Kerry – Pat Spillane, Tom Spillane, Ger Lynch

1990

This was the last of the 3-test series. Ireland won the series by 2–1 and by a margin of 24 points. There was an 8-year gap until the International Rules Series was revived.

Kerry – Jack O'Shea, Eoin Liston

1998

Ireland won the revived series under its new 2-match format by 10 points, managed by Meath's Colm O'Rourke.

Kerry – Seamus Moynihan

1999

Colm O'Rourke was back as manager again with his county man John McDermott as captain. Ireland won, this time by a margin of 8 points. The fact that the series win came in Australia made it all the sweeter.

Kerry – Seamus Moynihan, Declan O'Keeffe

2000

Donegal's Brian McEniff came in as manager, but this time around it was Australia who were very much in control. They eventually won the series by a comfortable margin of 25 points. Seamus Moynihan, Declan O'Keeffe and Darragh Ó Sé were the Kerry players involved and Meath's Trevor Giles was captain.

Kerry – Seamus Moynihan, Darragh Ó Sé, Declan O'Keeffe

2001

McEniff returned as manager in 2001 with Derry's Anthony Tohill as his captain. Ireland gained revenge after their millennium-year loss with a 25 point aggregate win, once again in Australia.

Kerry – Seamus Moynihan, Darragh Ó Sé, Mike Frank Russell, John Crowley, Tadhg Kennelly

2002

Kerry legend John O'Keeffe took over as manager with Seamus Moynihan captaining the side, but unfortunately for the Kerry duo it was the Aussies who won a tight series by an aggregate score of 7 points.

Kerry – Seamus Moynihan, Darragh Ó Sé, Tomás Ó Sé, Tadhg Kennelly

2003

John O'Keeffe returned as manager with Cork's Graeme Canty as captain. The Cork/Kerry alliance failed to produce a positive result, however, as Australia again won by 7 points, though this time they'd won a home series. There were no Kerry players in the travelling squad.

2004

Back in Ireland with Down's Pete McGrath as manager and Pádraic Joyce as captain, Ireland romped to a comfortable 50-point win.

Kerry – Tadhg Kennelly, Paul Galvin

2005

The same Down and Galway duo were back as manager and captain for the trip to Australia, but this time around the Aussies proved to be far too strong for the Irish. Having lost by 50 points the year previously, Australia went one better and won by 57 points. Crokes duo Eoin Brosnan and Colm Cooper were part of the Irish set-up for the first time.

Kerry – Eoin Brosnan, Colm Cooper, Tomás Ó Sé

2006

Meath's legendary manager Seán Boylan came on board as manager for this home series, with Armagh's All-Ireland-winning captain Kieran Mc-Geeney as captain. There was also a strong Kerry presence, including debutants Kieran Donaghy, Marc Ó Sé and Aidan O'Mahony. Unfortunately, Ireland lost the series by 30 points.

Kerry – Tadhg Kennelly, Paul Galvin, Kieran Donaghy, Marc Ó Sé, Aidan O'Mahony

2008

Boylan returned as manager in 2008 with Seán Cavanagh from Tyrone as captain for this latest trip to Australia. This proved to be a real crackerjack of a series with Ireland winning by the narrow margin of 5 points. Killian Young made his first international rules appearance in this series.

Kerry – Aidan O'Mahony, Killian Young, Kieran Donaghy

2010

Former Irish captain Anthony Tohill took over as Irish manager with Armagh's Steven McDonnell as captain. Kerry's Australian-based players Tommy Walsh and Tadhg Kennelly were both involved in what turned out to be a series loss by 10 points.

Kerry – Tommy Walsh, Tadhg Kennelly

2011

Tohill returned as manager for yet another trip down under with Dublin's All-Ireland-winning hero Stephen Cluxton as captain. This was a series which

Ireland completely controlled and they ended up winning by an aggregate score of 65 points. Kieran Donaghy travelled to Oz to join up with Tommy Walsh and Tadhg Kennelly. Kennelly, who had won an All-Ireland medal with Kerry 2 years previously, was appearing in his sixth International series and went on to be named Irish Player of the Series.

Kerry – Kieran Donaghy, Tommy Walsh, Tadhg Kennelly

2013

Another series and another new manager in the shape of Paul Earley from Roscommon. Earley had Michael Murphy of Donegal as his captain. There were no Kerry players involved in this series that Ireland won by an aggregate score of 101 points.

2014

The combination of Earley and Murphy were there again in 2014 when Ireland travelled to Australia. Kerry were of course All-Ireland champions that year but only David Moran was in the travelling party. Ireland lost the series by 10 points.

Kerry – David Moran

2015

By 2015 Armagh's Joe Kernan was the latest International Rules manager and he had Darragh Ó Sé as one of his selectors, while Bernard Brogan was team captain. This was the closest series of the past 20 years, with Ireland winning by just a 4-point aggregate. Once again there was minimum involvement from the Kerry camp, with just Colm Cooper as part of the squad.

Kerry – Colm Cooper

2017

Ireland travelled to Australia with Joe Kernan as manager and Mayo's Aidan O'Shea as captain. Peter Crowley, Paul Murphy and Paul Geaney were the latest Kerry players to wear the green singlet of Ireland in a tour, though unfortunately it ended in a 13-point defeat.

Kerry – Peter Crowley, Paul Murphy, Paul Geaney

5 Football Facts

1. Current Kerry Senior Football selector Maurice Fitzgerald was best man to current Kerry Senior Football manager Peter Keane at his wedding. The childhood friends played their Senior club football for St Mary's Cahersiveen together and both managed their club to Senior All-Ireland club titles in Croke Park.

2. Former Cork All Star Denny Long's best man at his wedding was Kerry's multiple All-Ireland medal winner, Mikey Sheehy. Sheehy and Long won an All-Ireland club medal together with Tralee club Austin Stacks. Denny Long hails from Millstreet in Cork just over the border, but has been based in Tralee for over 40 years.

3. Ned Fitzgerald captained South Kerry to county championship success in 1956, and 48 years later his son Maurice Fitzgerald captained South Kerry to the county title in 2004.

4. In 1988 Timmy Brosnan (St Kieran's) was the last captain to lift the old Bishop Moynihan

Cup, which is presented to the winners of the Senior County football championship in Kerry. In 1989 goalkeeper Peter Lyons (Laune Rangers) was the first man to lift the new Bishop Moynihan trophy, which is still in use today.

5. Former Dublin midfielder and star player Brian Mullins was the nephew of former Lispole and Kerry great Bill Casey.

ALL STARS

KERRY'S FOOTBALL ALL STAR WINNERS

The annual GAA All Star awards commenced back in 1971 and, as we head towards a new decade, the 50th anniversary of the inaugural awards will take place in 2021.

Since their inception back in 1971, Kerry have dominated the football awards. Donie O'Sullivan from the Spa club in Killarney was the first Kerry man to receive an All Star and Paul Galvin became the 1,000th All Star recipient.

Pat Spillane holds the record for most football award wins with 9.

When Kerry won the 4-in-a-row in 1981, 9 Kerry players won awards that year. Nine All Stars is the greatest amount that any county has won in a single year in Gaelic football.

Kerry's All Stars

1971:   Donie O'Sullivan

1972:   Donie O'Sullivan, Mick O'Connell

1973:   John O'Keeffe

1974:   Paudie Lynch

1975:   Ger Power, John O'Keeffe, John Egan, Paudie O'Mahony, Mickey O'Sullivan

1976:   Pat Spillane, Mikey Sheehy, Ger Power, John O'Keeffe, Ger O'Keeffe

1977:   Pat Spillane, John Egan

1978:   Pat Spillane, Mikey Sheehy, Ger Power, John O'Keeffe, John Egan, Paudie Lynch

1979:   Pat Spillane, Mikey Sheehy, Ger Power, John O'Keeffe, Tim Kennelly, Sean Walsh

1980:   Pat Spillane, Ger Power, Jack O'Shea, John Egan, Eoin Liston, Tim Kennelly, Charlie Nelligan

1981:   Pat Spillane, Mikey Sheehy, Jack O'Shea, Páidí Ó Sé, Eoin Liston, Paudie Lynch, Sean Walsh, Jimmy Deenihan, Denis Moran

1982:   Mikey Sheehy, Jack O'Shea, John Egan, Páidí Ó Sé, Eoin Liston

1983:   Jack O'Shea, Páidí Ó Sé

1984:   Pat Spillane, Mikey Sheehy, Jack O'Shea, Páidí Ó Sé, Eoin Liston, Tommy Doyle, Tom Spillane

1985:   Pat Spillane, Jack O'Shea, Páidí Ó Sé, Tommy Doyle, Mick Spillane

1986:   Pat Spillane, Mikey Sheehy, Ger Power, Tommy Doyle, Tom Spillane, Charlie Nelligan

1987:   Tom Spillane, Ger Lynch

1988:   Maurice Fitzgerald

1989:   Connie Murphy

1996:   Maurice Fitzgerald

1997:   Maurice Fitzgerald, Declan O'Keeffe, Seamus Moynihan, Eamonn Breen, Pa Laide

2000:   Declan O'Keeffe, Seamus Moynihan, Mike McCarthy, Darragh Ó Sé, Liam Hassett, Mike Frank Russell

2001:   Johnny Crowley

2002:   Darragh Ó Sé, Colm Cooper

2004:   Diarmuid Murphy, Tom O'Sullivan, Mike McCarthy, Tomás Ó Sé, Paul Galvin, Colm Cooper

2005:   Diarmuid Murphy, Mike McCarthy, Tomás Ó Sé, Colm Cooper

2006:   Marc Ó Sé, Seamus Moynihan, Aidan

O'Mahony, Darragh Ó Sé, Paul Galvin, Kieran Donaghy

2007: Marc Ó Sé, Tomás Ó Sé, Aidan O'Mahony, Darragh Ó Sé, Declan O'Sullivan, Colm Cooper

2008: Tomás Ó Sé, Declan O'Sullivan, Colm Cooper, Kieran Donaghy

2009: Diarmuid Murphy, Tom O'Sullivan, Tomás Ó Sé, Séamus Scanlon, Paul Galvin, Tadhg Kennelly, Declan O'Sullivan

2010: Colm Cooper

2011: Marc Ó Sé, Bryan Sheehan, Darran O'Sullivan, Colm Cooper

2013: Colm Cooper, James O'Donoghue

2014: Paul Murphy, Peter Crowley, David Moran, Kieran Donaghy, James O'Donoghue

2015: Brendan Kealy, Shane Enright, Anthony Maher, Donnchadh Walsh

2016: Paul Geaney

2017: Paul Geaney

2018: David Clifford

141 All Stars won in total

HIGHEST NUMBER OF ALL STARS WON BY KERRY PLAYERS

9   Pat Spillane

8   Colm Cooper

7   Mikey Sheehy

6   Jack O'Shea, Ger Power

5   John O'Keeffe, John Egan, Páidí Ó Sé, Tomás Ó Sé

4   Eoin Liston, Darragh Ó Sé

3   Paudie Lynch, Tommy Doyle, Tom Spillane, Maurice Fitzgerald, Seamus Moynihan, Mike McCarthy, Diarmuid Murphy, Paul Galvin, Marc Ó Sé, Kieran Donaghy, Declan O'Sullivan

2   Donie O'Sullivan, Tim Kennelly, Sean Walsh, Charlie Nelligan, Declan O'Keeffe, Tom O'Sullivan, Aidan O'Mahony, James O'Donoghue, Paul Geaney

1   Mick O'Connell, Paudie O'Mahony, Mickey Ned O'Sullivan, Ger O'Keeffe, Denis Moran, Jimmy Deenihan, Mick Spillane, Ger Lynch, Connie Murphy, Eamonn Breen, Pa Laide, Liam Hassett, Mike Frank Russell, John Crowley, Séamus

Scanlon, Tadhg Kennelly, Bryan Sheehan, Darran O'Sullivan, Paul Murphy, Peter Crowley, David Moran, Brendan Kealy, Shane Enright, Anthony Maher, Donnchadh Walsh, David Clifford

Team of Kerry All Stars

A team of Kerry All Stars based on the 15 men who have won the most awards.

Diarmuid Murphy (3)

Páidí Ó Sé (5)   John O'Keeffe (5)   Marc Ó Sé (3)

Tomás Ó Sé (5) Seamus Moynihan (3) Ger Power (6)

Jack O'Shea (6)   Darragh Ó Sé (4)

Maurice (3)   Colm Cooper (8)   Pat Spillane (9)
Fitzgerald

Mikey Sheehy (7)   Eoin Liston (4)   John Egan (5)

Subs: Paudie Lynch, Tommy Doyle, Tom Spillane, Mike McCarthy, Paul Galvin, Kieran Donaghy, Declan O'Sullivan (all 3)

LADIES FOOTBALL ALL STARS

The annual Ladies Football All Star awards commenced back in 1980. Kerry's first All Star winners were Eileen O'Connor, Eileen Lawlor and Mary Jo Curran.

The inaugural Ladies awards came just before a period where Kerry dominated the Ladies game. They won a phenomenal 9-in-a-row of All-Ireland Senior titles between 1982 and 1990 and that was duly recognised in the All Star ceremonies.

Mary Jo Curran went on to win 11 awards, a record that she shares with Mayo's Cora Staunton, who won her 11th All Star in 2017.

Curran won a phenomenal 8-in-a-row from 1983 to 1990, which is another All Star record.

Kerry have won 88 All Stars in the 38-year history of the awards, with 31 different winners.

Kerry Ladies All Star Winners

11　Mary Jo Curran (1980–81, 1983–90, 1993)

6　Marina Barry (1986–87, 1989, 1991–93)

5　Eileen Lawlor (1980, 1983–84, 1988, 1990),

Margaret Lawlor (1982, 1984–85, 1988, 1990), Bridget Leen (1984, 1990–92, 1994), Kathleen Curran (1985–88, 1994), Geraldine O'Shea (1995–96, 2002–04)

4   Del Whyte (1982, 1985–87), Annette Walsh (1983, 1987–89), Marion Doherty (1984–85, 1989–90)

3   Mary Twomey (1981–83), Phil Curran (1988–89, 1991), Katie Liston (1990–91, 1993), Fionnuala Ruane (1992–93, 1995)

2   Eileen O'Connor (1980–81), Marie Fitzgerald (1993, 1995), Sarah O'Connor (2001, 2006), Sarah Houlihan (2012–13), Louise Ní Mhuircheartaigh (2012–13)

1   Hilda O'Leary (1982), Nora Foley (1983), Lil O'Sullivan (1985), Nora Hallissey (1986), Mary Lane (1987), Andrea O'Donoghue (2003), Kacey O'Driscoll (2003), Edel Murphy (2010), Cait Lynch (2012), Aislinn Desmond (2015), Caroline Kelly (2017), Lorraine Scanlon (2017)

5 Football Facts

1. When Kerry won the All-Ireland Senior Football titles in 1969 and 1984, the sub goalkeepers were club mates of the starting keepers. Weeshie Fogarty and Johnny Culloty (Killarney Legion) in 1969, and Tom Lynch and Charlie Nelligan (Castleisland Desmonds) in 1984.

2. In 1965 Derry and John (Thorny) O'Shea were the only brothers in history to be sent off on the same day in an All-Ireland final.

3. John Egan was the Offaly captain in 1969 when Kerry won the All-Ireland Senior football final and his namesake, the late John Egan, was the Kerry captain when Offaly denied Kerry the 5-in-a-row in the 1982 final.

4. Ogie Moran was the Kerry team mascot in the 1962 All-Ireland Senior Football final, and he went on to win a record-equalling 8 All-Ireland Senior medals, as well as captaining Kerry to All-Ireland Senior glory in 1978. Colm Cooper

was the mascot for Dr Crokes in the 1992 All-Ireland Senior club football final, and 25 years on he won an All-Ireland Senior club medal for the Crokes.

5. Pat and Mick Spillane won Senior All-Ireland medals in 1980 and their younger brother, Tom, won an All-Ireland Minor medal on the same day. The 3 brothers went on to win a total of 19 Senior All-Ireland medals between them, which is a record for one family.

VOICES OF
KERRY GAA

THE MEN WITH
THE MICROPHONE

Kerry commentators have brought the game of football to life over the years for so many radio listeners and TV viewers who, for whatever reason, are not able to attend our games. The following is a tribute to some of these men who have left such a lasting legacy over the years.

Mícheál Ó Muircheartaigh

The advent of GAA broadcasting only really took place in the past 70 years or so. Television became an integral part of GAA championship coverage in the 1960s, but before that supporters would gather around the wireless to listen to RTÉ's match commentary. Mícheál Ó Muircheartaigh, from Dingle, was the voice of national GAA radio commentary for over 6 decades.

Mícheál was born in Dún Síon just outside Dingle in 1930 and is of course a fluent Irish speaker. In early March 1949, he, along with other students, did a test commentary on a hurling game at Croke Park and the rest, as they say, is history.

His first assignment was to provide an all-Irish commentary on the 1949 Railway Cup final.

Mícheál's multi-award-winning career stretched to 2010 when he officially retired as a GAA commentator, but the West Kerry man has kept highly active and is still regularly involved in projects associated with the GAA.

Weeshie Fogarty

The word 'legend' is often used far too liberally, but Weeshie Fogarty was without doubt a broadcasting genius and is a name that is synonymous with the GAA in the county.

A psychiatric nurse by profession, Weeshie lived most of his adult life just a kick of a ball away from Fitzgerald Stadium. He played football with his club Killarney Legion, East Kerry and Kerry. He was a renowned goalkeeper in his day, winning All-Ireland Junior medals with Kerry, and was also sub goalie to Johnny Culloty with the Kerry Seniors for a period of time. In later years, he was also a top-class referee.

Later in life, Weeshie became best known for his work in radio and won multiple awards for his ground-breaking show *Terrace Talk*. His co-

commentary at matches also became the thing of legend, as he used all his wit and knowledge to paint a picture for the listeners at home. Weeshie was a broadcasting natural and a never-to-be-forgotten voice of Kerry GAA.

Liam Higgins

The late Liam will first and foremost be remembered for his deeds on the football field with his club Lispole, his District West Kerry and of course his county. Liam was a member of the Kerry Senior inter-county team from 1969 until 1973 and he won 2 Senior All-Ireland medals. After retiring, he managed Lispole and West Kerry, and he also managed the Kerry Junior team to Munster and All-Ireland glory in 1983. Liam was a teacher by profession and in that capacity he also trained Dingle CBS to 2 All-Ireland Championships in 1996 and 2001.

Liam was the first GAA commentator for Radio Kerry sport and in his time with the station he struck up a remarkable partnership with Weeshie Fogarty. The duo gained fame far and wide for their match-day commentaries and were simply known as the voices of Kerry GAA. Liam's knowledge of the game and passion for all things Kerry were delivered over the airwaves to the 4 corners of the county and beyond. He continued to broadcast right up to his untimely death in 2006.

Mícheál Ó Sé

West Kerry have produced some memorable commentators over the years and Mícheál Ó Sé is certainly one of them. He has graced the national airwaves for many a year.

Mícheál was also, of course, a Kerry Senior footballer of note. He was born in Ard na Caithne, in the Gaeltacht in West Kerry in 1946. Mícheál was on the Kerry Senior inter-county team from 1968 to 1976, winning 2 All-Ireland Senior medals during that time. He also won an All-Ireland medal with the Kerry Minors and a 1976 club junior county championship title.

Mícheál provided commentary in Irish for RTÉ's *The Sunday Game* and also appeared on Raidió na Gaeltachta, where he had his own show, *Saol Ó Dheas*. He is probably most famous for his vivid commentaries in Irish of the All-Ireland Minor finals over the years.

Gary O'Sullivan

The Portmagee native was very much the voice of the Radio Kerry sport department from 2004 up to 2018, when he announced that he was leaving his post in Radio Kerry to pursue other interests. Gary took over the live commentary on Senior inter-county games after Liam Higgins' sad passing in 2006, and he established himself as a highly respected commentator who brought the game to life in a period where Kerry won 4 Senior All-Ireland football titles.

Gary has a wide depth of knowledge on all sports and he also presented the weekend sports programme on Radio Kerry, which proved to be very popular with local listeners. He has been heavily involved with his local football club, Skellig Rangers, and the highlight of his time in radio came when Skellig Rangers won the All-Ireland Junior Club title in Croke Park in 2009.

Tim Moynihan

The Knocknagoshel native is the current presenter of the renowned *Terrace Talk* programme on Radio Kerry. Tim took over from the late Weeshie Fogarty 3 years ago and has brought his own inimitable style of broadcasting to the programme.

Tim is also the main match-day commentator for Radio Kerry sport, having replaced the recently retired Gary O'Sullivan. Tim is well known now for his high octane commentary and was recently nominated for the Sports Broadcaster of the Year Award at the IMRO National Radio Awards.

Pádraig Ó Sé

The man from the west has been commentating on GAA *as Gaeilge* for RTÉ for nearly 2 decades. Pádraig's poetic commentary is a joy to listen to. He is also a renowned musician and is well known for his television work with TG4.

Pádraig follows in the footsteps of fellow west-born commentators like Mícheál Ó Muircheartaigh, Mícheál Ó Sé and Liam Higgins. There must be something in the water back west!

Pádraig's sons, Tomás and Óigí, both play with their local club, An Ghaeltacht. Tomás won an All-Ireland Minor medal with Kerry and is a noted Irish dancer. As well as commentating, Pádraig has hosted TV shows such as *Bean an Tí sa Chistin* and *Feis and Blood*.

Ger O'Connor

The Glenbeigh native has been a commentator with Radio Kerry for over a decade. O'Connor was the match-day commentator for the Kerry Minors' great run of recent success, but probably his greatest day with the microphone came when his club, Glenbeigh/Glencar, captured the All-Ireland Junior title in Croke Park in 2017.

Ger is also renowned as a *seanchaí*, and he undoubtedly brings that ability to tell a story to his match-day commentary. He also provides coverage of local GAA games for Radio Kerry.

EPILOGUE

While Dublin might be the kingpins of Senior football right now, the Kerry Minors have just completed an historic 5-in-a-row and Kerry have also won an historic 4-in-a-row at Junior level. Jimmy Keane's Juniors will be looking to make it back-to-back 5-in-a-rows for the county in 2019.

That's the true secret of Kerry football. At all levels, success follows success, whether it be underage, Colleges, Junior or Senior, as well as at club level in every grade. The conveyor belt of talent is undoubtedly turning stronger than ever, despite what some commentators might say.

Peter Keane has taken over from Eamonn Fitzmaurice as Kerry Senior football manager and he has assembled an all-star back-room team that includes Maurice Fitzgerald, Donie Buckley, Tommy Griffin and James Foley.

Kerry supporters will go to all 4 corners of Ireland to follow their county's footballers, but, much as we love the green and gold army, they expect success.

Fortunately, history tells us Kerry will not be in

the doldrums at Senior level for long. 'The Famine', as the barren period without a Senior All-Ireland title between 1986 and 1997 became known, is the longest time that Kerry have had to wait for an All-Ireland title since winning their first back in 1903. Their total of 37 victories in 115 years means that Kerry have won an All-Ireland Senior title roughly every 3 years on average.

Our last Senior title came back in 2014, so the law of averages certainly suggests that Kerry's 38th All-Ireland Senior title cannot be that far away.

Ciarraí Abú.

REFERENCES

Books

Barry, John & Horan, Eamon, *Years of Glory: The Story of Kerry's All-Ireland Senior Victories* (The Kerryman, Tralee, 1977)

Connolly, Kieran, *Sam Maguire: The Man and the Cup* (Mercier Press, Cork, 2017)

Donegan, Des, *The Complete Handbook of Gaelic Games 1887–2005* (DBA Publications Ltd, Dublin, 2005)

Horgan, Tim, *Fighting for the Cause* (Mercier Press, Cork, 2018)

McElligott, Richard, *Forging a Kingdom: The GAA in Kerry 1884–1934* (Collins Press, Cork, 2013)

Ó Muircheartaigh, Joe & Flynn, T. J., *Princes of Pigskin: A Century of Kerry Footballers* (Collins Press, Cork, 2007)

Websites

www.terracetalk.com
www.gaa.ie
www.munstergaa.ie
www.wikipedia.org
www.kerryladiesfootball.com
www.kerrygaa.ie

ACKNOWLEDGEMENTS

A project like this would not have been possible without the support of my family. I want to thank the most important people in my life: my wife Helena and my teenagers, Cillian and Eve, for all their advice and patience but most of all their love.

A number of people played important roles in getting this publication to print:

To all my colleagues at *Kerry's Eye*, I want to thank you for your support and professionalism. To my former sports editor and confidant, Jim O'Gorman, for being first and foremost a great friend but also a good man for offering advice and wise counsel.

Kerry GAA historian and Vice-Chairman of Kerry Coiste na nÓg, Tadhg O'Halloran, has also been a great friend and he provided me with so much information for this publication. Tadhg is an endless source of information on Kerry GAA.

Austin Stacks club man and another noted Kerry GAA historian, Tim Slattery, has also been a great source of information. Thank you Tim for all your help.

Many thanks to everyone on the publishing team of Mercier Press. To Noel O'Regan in particular – Noel approached me with the original idea for this Kerry GAA football supporters' guide. Noel is of course a Tralee man and the grandson of Kerry All-Ireland Senior medal winner Martin 'Bracker' O'Regan. Noel has been my right-hand man throughout this process.

I would also like to thank my great friend Peter Keane for his kind words. The Kerry Senior Football manager's endorsement has been gratefully received.

Last but not least, I would like to pay tribute to the wonderful Kerry football supporters. I have enjoyed many a day in your company at GAA grounds all over the country. Nothing beats supporting the various Kerry inter-county teams. Kerry supporters are passionate, colourful, vocal but more than anything, they are knowledgeable and fair.

ABOUT THE AUTHOR

Sylvester Hennessy is the sports editor with *Kerry's Eye*. A renowned GAA statistician, he appears regularly on Radio Kerry to discuss all things Kerry football. He was also a member of the back-room team for the Kerry Minor footballers' recent historic 5-in-a-row All-Ireland victory.